Anything For You

One Woman's Unrelenting

Journey to Motherhood

Written By: Christina Rios

Copyright © 2020 by Christina Rios

All Rights Reserved.

ISBN: 9798594840270

Table of Contents

1. THE BEGINNING.. 6
2. THE LAPAROSCOPY.. 27
3. ITS BABY-MAKING TIME!... 39
4. THE WAIT.. 44
5. THE FIRST TRIMESTER... 55
6. THE SECOND TRIMESTER.. 69
7. THIRD TRIMESTER.. 85
8. BABY SHOWER TIME!... 99
9. WHAT HAPPENS NEXT.. 105
10. THE AFTERMATH... 113
11. LEAVING THE HOSPITAL WITHOUT HIM................... 118
12. FINALLY HOME.. 123
13. LASER WHAT?.. 130
14. HOW IS MOMMY?.. 134
15. UPDATES!.. 142
16. ACKNOWLEDGEMENTS... 145

4
- *Something special happens to everyone at least one time in his or her life – Christina Rios*

Dedicated to my little man Isaiah,

You are the reason for it all. Mommy loves you so so much!

The Beginning

June 2, 2012

Who knew that after all this time, I would be walking into a fertility clinic for the first time ever for a consultation? That's right! I said it! I am going to start making us a baby! There are so many questions! How long will this take? What is the first step? How do we choose a donor? Where do we look? Why haven't I gotten pregnant before? Was there something wrong with me? Before I knew it I was being called into the office and so it all begins...

My wife, Denise and I had it all. We both had good jobs, a decent home in a nice area, and a strong foundation for our marriage. It all started when I began working for a telecommunications company. I am naturally a loner. I always sit back and observe before I can comfortably begin interacting with you. It is in my nature as an introvert. During training, I sat in the second to last seat hoping nobody would sit there and I would have extra space to stretch out and place my bags. Just as our first training class began, she walks in and hurries to the back of the room, pulls out the seat behind me and makes herself comfortable with her energy drink in hand. I remember giving her one of those looks where I didn't think she was serious since there were so many other free seats that had been left available. She and I really did not speak at first. Days went by and little by little we began talking to each other.

It started with a simple "Good Morning" and an occasional "How are you?" It wasn't until one morning she had to leave the training room due to having heart palpitations that she and I really began conversing. The trainer had asked me to bring Denise her belongings and sit with her until the ambulance arrived. I tried making light of the moment by telling her she should have listened when I warned her about consuming those energy drinks so frequently. Eventually after sitting in a classroom for 8 hours a day, everyone began building bonds, carpooling, taking lunch breaks together etc. She was very easygoing and free spirited. She spoke her mind and has always been very witty. I grew to enjoy it and allowed myself to interact with her even though I was still skeptical. In my eyes she was also a bit cocky and that made me withdraw a bit. However boredom kicked in and jokes were being tossed around the room. Soon after it seemed as though we were all back in high school, and constantly being told to quiet down or to stop talking. It was funny and even now I am smiling thinking back on those moments.

    One day during our break, I was writing something in my journal (I used to carry a book with me everywhere). I had just happened to be writing a poem. From that moment a door opened and we began talking more and more, getting to know each other. We would pass sticky notes back and forth all throughout the day. To be frank, I was beginning to really enjoy her company. She may argue this down with me until she is blue in the face however she initiated the first move! She offered to take me home one day, as I did not drive. I am a city girl from NYC. I took the trains everywhere! We realized we only lived about fifteen minutes from each other, so I agreed. We made small talk on the way home and it was cool. The next day, she picked me up and it became routine for her to ride me to and from work.

One evening, she asked me out to dinner, as coworkers and I obliged. We went to Chevy's in Linden NJ and it became a weekly tradition ever since. The first night we had dinner made all the difference. It was so much fun and we both had one too many but we went our separate ways and immediately started texting each other when she got home that evening. I was actually planning to go to my friends All White Affair for his first book release the upcoming weekend and I needed advice on how my dress looked. So I tried it on, took a picture and sent it to several friends, one of which was Denise. She still believes to this day that it was I making a move but I was truly just looking for comments on the outfit. It was a very short figure fitting off white colored dress with long sleeves and I wore thigh high brown boots with it. As messages from different friends and my sister poured in, I found myself skipping all of those for her message. She replied with one word, "Damn." So it was from that moment I knew I would wear the outfit and thanked her for her feedback. We went back and forth in text message after that and her comments led me to believe there was more behind that "Damn" than I originally thought. What I did not originally admit is that I kind of liked it. I had never been with a woman before so I was also intimidated, not that it had crossed my mind in that moment but I was becoming a bit curious… I ended up asking her straight out if she was bisexual or into women. She did not answer right away. As time went on I invited her to my place, just to chill. We watched television; I introduced her to new musical artists like Chrisette Michele and Robin Thicke. It was a really good evening. I felt so comfortable and free. The vibe was definitely a smooth one. She ended up sleeping over that evening and basically never left. I gave her a key shortly after and that is when we began our journey together. It was October 11th. We often took trips down to Florida or Georgia and so many other places. We were enjoying life and exploring new things together.

She proposed to me a couple of years later in the Grand Cayman Islands. It was magical! We went swimming in the middle of the ocean with stingrays and then swam with dolphins. Later that evening she planned a romantic dinner on the beach. Rose petals led us to a table secluded just by the ocean. We ate a lovely four-course meal and I experienced the joy of an apple martini for the first time. I remember us sitting there, our bellies full as can be looking out at the ocean and listening to the waves. She began telling me how she felt about me and what she wanted for us. Right when I looked at her she looked down at a red box sitting on the table. My heart raced and my full attention was on her and the love she was verbally expressing for us and for me. Then she asked and I said YES!

I was so full of love and life the entire time. She had a way of bringing the best out of people. She is so intelligent and goal oriented. Just being around her made me want to do more for myself. I felt that if I were going to love this woman I had to be right and I had to do it the right way. I will always cherish her for making me want to seek the best life has to offer just by being around her. This is what made me fall in love with her. She and I came from two different backgrounds and had two very different visions of what life should be but there was never any judgment. Only when she was cracking jokes on me but I did not mind. I have also always been very witty. Together we fit perfectly in the puzzle of life. We ended up getting married on October 22, just a year after the engagement. That night was so full of emotions, unconditional love and so many memories. It was everything a wedding night should be and so much more.

We came to a point where we were tired of the ripping and running, hitting lounges or restaurants for happy hours. We used to go to Friday's on Tuesday and Thursday nights because our favorite DJ was there and the music was always on point. There is only so much partying you can do before you realize it gets old pretty fast. Soon enough you would much rather be at home watching movies or just talking and spending quality time together.

After discussing it for some time, we decided to add another person to the party. It was time. We wanted to have a little munchkin to call our own. Denise really didn't want to be pregnant (She said the only way that would happen is if she can be pregnant for only three months, which didn't seem plausible). Anyway, my wife has low tolerance for pain and anytime something out of the ordinary happens to her body, she freaks out. She becomes the biggest baby when she catches even the slightest cold. I could only imagine the hell it would have been to take care of her while she was pregnant. It was clear she was not ready to have a growing belly, although I do still think she would look so adorable pregnant, and I figured, I was in good health so I would carry our bundle of joy.

We started off by researching. We researched different procedures on how to get pregnant; during this process we learned a lot of information. Maybe even a bit too much information if you ask me. Some of it was really scary. For example, we quickly learned that this would not be a one two three process... There would be a plethora of medical testing involved even before getting pregnant. Some websites indicated it could take years to get pregnant. It would also cost a lot of money, because insurance really doesn't cover much. Yes, I already called to get an idea of what this would cost us out of pocket. I had so many questions. How quickly would I become pregnant? Is artificial insemination the same as intrauterine insemination?

Why do they call it artificial insemination? In my opinion there really isn't anything artificial about the process. The only difference in my opinion is the tool that is used to inject the sperm. Just because there isn't a penis involved doesn't make it any less of a reproduction process. At this point in my research, this is where I am beginning to think the world still has a lot of growing to do. People are still so closed-minded. It really makes it unfair to not only those of us in same sex relationships but to women who do have a difficult time conceiving. It is the little things like calling our process "artificial" that really bugs me. I wont get into the politics of it all although I do believe I bring up a valid point.

Anyway, after spending countless hours on the computer, and calling different specialists, and our insurance companies; discussing costs and timing, we picked a specialist close by. We set up the appointment for a consultation and we prayed, A LOT. We kept this part of our journey a secret because we didn't want to jinx anything. In the Hispanic culture we believe in "mal de ojo" which is a basic term for the "Evil Eye." I am Puerto Rican and the evil eye suggests that when people are jealous of you, it creates a negative energy.

There are times where you may see people wearing a red bracelet with (or sometimes without) an eye in the middle. This is believed to keep bad energy and evil wishes away from you. We simply did not want any jealousy or people in our business, at least for the time being. I was also brought up believing that if I want something bad enough, I have to keep it to myself. This was something I had always carried with me by watching my mother grow up and raise five children on her own. On top of which, my wife is very private so with respect to her wishes as well as my own beliefs, we kept our fertility journey to ourselves.

The first step was seeing a specialist, not because I had any infertility issues but because I am in a same sex marriage. We needed guidance on where to start and what our options were.

We ended up picking a fertility specialist literally right across the street from us. The convenience was a relief, especially considering how nervous I had become thinking about the rest of it. As we sat waiting to see the fertility specialist for my consultation, I was riddled with anxiety. I had no idea what to expect and it occurred to me that maybe it would be difficult for me to get pregnant, even with the ideal donor sperm. I had been in a heterosexual relationship before in which we engaged in unprotected sex and yet I had not gotten pregnant. Did this mean I was infertile? So many thoughts and questions started shooting through my mind.

The office was large and there was ample seating available, although we were the only ones there. I sat in one of the brown wooden seats waiting to be called. Denise sat next to me and began pulling brochures out from everywhere she possibly could. News played on the television, which was mounted on the wall. The wall was a light blue, which I found comforting, even if just momentarily. There was a picture of the beach hanging right next to the TV and a picture of a mother holding a baby in a frame on the adjacent wall. The mother and her baby jolted me once more, and the longer I sat there; the more I began to process the fact that there may very well be something wrong with me. Why hadn't I become pregnant before? Maybe it simply was not my time, but what if there is something truly wrong? My thoughts overwhelmed me, and my anxiety was reaching crescendo.

Just as I felt myself getting ready to burst into tears with thinking there may be an issue with me, I heard the nurse call my name. So many questions were popping up in my head as Denise and I walked into the doctor's office. His desk was full of paperwork and folders. A huge calendar sat right in the middle of all the paperwork, and a few different models of the vaginal canal, uterus and other anatomy were on display. The large dark wooden desk and two chairs placed directly in front of it took up most of the space in the office. He also had two different computer screens on the side of his desk and a cabinet that rested along the wall with huge windows. I later found out this file cabinet held brochures, magnets promoting the office along with note pads and other things he pulled out as he made his way to his chair. Although my mind was racing nonstop, I remember sitting there quietly listening to him explain what he does and how he can help us.

    He asked some questions about my health, family history, eating habits and past relationships. The conversation was personal and detailed. When I noted my concern about not previously getting pregnant, he said that we would do some tests, but it wasn't something to worry about at this point. I was going to have to do blood work along with other testing to make sure I was physically able to go through with the intrauterine insemination (IUI) process. Basically, IUI is like using a turkey baster to inseminate yourself, but with a medical professional and medical tools. IUI is both less invasive and less expensive than in vitro fertilization (IVF). Denise and I both agreed this would be the best option to start with.

Appointments were set for my blood work and a scheduled outpatient procedure as well a Hysterosalpingogram (HSG). The doctor explained that an HSG exam was the first step in determining if other procedures, such as the more invasive laparoscopy would be warranted. After setting up the appointments, we were given brochures to look for potential donors. There were many different offices and websites to choose from so we had our work cut out for us. Even if you know your sperm donor and you use a turkey baster, there is still so much risk involved. How well do you really know your donor, anyway? Do you know if he has a family history of heart disease? Does he have a good education? What about how much involvement he would have in the child's life? How much involvement did we want him to have? For us, using an anonymous donor simplified the equation.

    Fertility clinics offer genetic testing, and you get to choose anonymous donors by sifting through the albums that include family medical histories and baby pictures. They also have plenty of reputable donor websites that allow these same options. This allows you to get a history of the donor, their blood type, and to better imagine what your future child might look like. They often include photos of the donor allowing you to see what he looked like as a baby up until adulthood. I wanted to know the blood type and family history of the donor because the pieces needed to fit. I wanted to be as prepared as possible.

    I felt comfortable with this specialist. He answered all of our questions and was very upfront about it all. I had hope. I was focused on being a mother and being lucky enough to give all of my love to this little tiny baby who I imagined holding and kissing every time I closed my eyes. Would I have a girl or a boy? Would the baby look like the donor or me? What donor would we choose? There were so many questions that I wanted answered but we had to decide on a place to begin looking first! My wife and I spent a few days going online and looking at reviews for the potential cryobanks. The hard part was comparing the quality of the specimen. We had to keep in mind we were looking for someone who had a high rate in successful pregnancies. We were looking for someone who had the same blood type as me. What about family history? Family history is very important as well. There were so many things to take into consideration.

June 27, 2012
Happy birthday to me! I am treating myself to a $375.00 three-month subscription of unlimited donor viewing!
Haha!
This is awesome! I never knew stuff like this existed until now. So many choices yet so little time. Did I mention endless questions? Will the baby look like the donor or me? Which nationality should we choose? Do donor hobbies even matter? It is not like those habits or likes would be passed down to the baby... Right? Why are some donors more expensive than others? Who shows baby pics but not adult pics? This is torture! Just kidding, we are enjoying this but I must say, I am a bit overwhelmed.

The cryobank we finally chose provided us with everything we needed to make a sound decision on the donor we were looking for. It had everything from baby pictures to medical and family history, right down to psychiatric evaluations. We even got to see what the donors' handwriting looked like and heard their interviews as to why they chose to be donors. It was really fascinating.

Now that we found the cryobank, we had to decide on characteristics. Which nationality were we going to go with? Could we find someone who shared the same physical characteristics as me? Or maybe a little bit of the both of us? Would this increase our chances of the baby looking like one of us? With so many arising questions we had no clue on where to start. So we just started clicking on random donors. We looked at every person who caught our eyes for one reason or another.

We looked at countless medical records and read a number of essays from the donors. Some essays included what the donors' interests were or why they decided to become a donor. For example, one donor went on about the history of his education and how he is family oriented while another donor expressed his love for music and breakdancing. One donor in particular mentioned that he wanted to help families who were having infertility issues. It was intriguing to learn that donors sometimes tend to think about some of things we do when looking for specimen. Some of the essays were well written while others had handwriting that was illegible. What turned us off was the lack of information some of the donors provided. Some donors seemed to oversell themselves as well. We even had access to pictures. Some donors only had baby pictures while others showed us what they looked like throughout adulthood. We learned that donors had preferences as well. Some of them didn't wish to be contacted until the child turns 18 years of age and even then, we would have to go through the cryobank to see if they are still interested in meeting the child. Other donors didn't wish to be contacted at all. This was also something we would have to take into consideration. That is when it hit us.

At some point in our child's life he or she will want to know how they were created, who their biological father is, and where he is. Will they want to meet him? Thinking of this brought up so many other questions. How will our child feel once they learn they have two mommies? Would this cause issues for him or her in school? What if having two mommies isn't enough? Surely my spouse and I were prepared to love this child unconditionally but what we were not prepared for was feeling inadequate or even answering these types of questions. What would we tell our baby? Would our child be hurt in any kind of way from learning the donor will not be in their day-to-day lives? There is already so much to consider when bringing a child into this world.

One thing is for sure, the more I thought about my future as a mother the more I realized that I would be okay. Growing up, I watched my mother raise five children all on her own. There were ups and downs and times where she didn't seem to have the energy to keep going but she never stopped. She kept moving forward with each day and had confidence in herself as a woman and a mother. That made all the difference. Observing other mothers throughout my life, I realized how hard they worked simply to see a smile on their child's face. The common denominator in this equation was love and lots of it. I already cared so much about this child and his or her feelings, long before my munchkin even existed. Yes, worrying about all of this is natural, I was learning this and it confirmed for me, that I was ready.

And then, we found him. He seemed perfect. His baby pictures were the cutest, his blood type matched mine, he had a high rating at successful pregnancies, and his family history seemed to be good as well. He was the most adorable brown skinned baby I had ever seen with dark big brown eyes and lots of hair. He didn't have any pictures from his adulthood or teenage years but Denise so desperately wanted to choose him! We were both excited to find him. There was only one issue. There was a waiting list for his specimen. We really didn't have time to be placed on a waiting list since we were beginning the process right away. When we called the cryobank to see how long the wait list would be, they confirmed it could be six months or longer. They explained the reason it took so long is because donors had to be tested over again after a certain amount of time to ensure safety for not only the person purchasing the specimen but to ensure the specimen itself held up to their standards. Disappointed we added ourselves to the wait list and continued searching.

Not too long after our disappointing let down of the first choice, we found another potential donor. This donor shared so many similar hobbies and everything else seemed to align with our requests. His blood type was the same as mine, his family history and psychiatric evaluations were all good, and he also has a very high rating for successful pregnancies. We found out he loved to dance, he loved music and he played football in high school. We even got to see pictures from when he was a baby to his adulthood, which is something we both appreciated. There was a picture of him in his football uniform as a teen. He has so adorable as a baby and we both found him to be an attractive man with thick curly hair. He was also very tall. The thing that caught my eye the most was his honesty. He was completely honest about why he chose to become a sperm donor. His answer was quite comical and that was enough for us. When asked why he wanted to become a donor, his response was "I need the money." His voice was deep and he sounded young but was well spoken. He seemed to be full of life and wanted to help other people create families of their own. The fact that he was also witty brought comfort in making a decision. So we made our choice.

    I am a firm believer in everything happening for a reason. Once we purchased the specimen and had it shipped off to the fertility clinic, we felt like we were finally getting somewhere. Pretty much as soon as the shipment was confirmed through our fertility clinic, we received a call from the cryobank that our first choice had just become available for purchase. That was an "aha" moment for me. I knew in my heart then that the decision we made was meant to be. For the specimen of our first choice to be unavailable to us until we had chosen someone else confirmed in my spirit that our first choice for some reason was not the right choice. I felt complete and was now ready to confidently take the next step in this journey.

The Laparoscopy

September 2012

Well, Today I had my HSG done. To be frank, I am not sure how I feel. It has been an uncomfortable day for me altogether. I am totally ready to just take it down for the night. Today is the first day that I feel exhausted from this whole baby making process. Not exhausted in the sense that I'm running too much, but in the sense of me allowing my thoughts to consume me. You know? *Sighs*

Tomorrow I meet with the fertility specialist again, so we shall see...

The first procedure I had to endure was the HSG, which is an imaging test to see if the fallopian tubes are blocked. Essentially, the fertility specialist needs to see what he is working with, so to speak. I had to go to a different office for the exam, which already made me anxious. This office was much less inviting. The walls were painted an ugly yellow, and there were blue chairs that reminded me of being in the waiting room at the hospital emergency room. The secretary sat behind the glass chewing away at the gum in her mouth, ordering people to sign in and give her their insurance card when they walked in. I greeted her with a good morning and she just barely looked up to acknowledge me before continuing to do what she was doing. She handed me a clipboard to fill out without so much as even looking at me.

"Do you want me to hold this for you? Or did you want me to fill it out and return it to you?" I asked sarcastically. I was nervous and she certainly wasn't helping. She ignored my questions and handed me a pen, pointing to the seating area.

It wasn't long before they called me into the room and asked me to undress. "Do I even get breakfast first?" I joked. The nurse just shot a cold look in my direction and asked me to wait for the doctor as she closed the door, leaving me alone in the cold room. The only things in the room were a large machine, a table to lay just under the machine, and a monitor that was off to the corner. As I waited for the doctor, I stared at this huge machine in front of me. I wasn't sure what it did or how it worked but if sending chills down my spine was part of the process, then it was successful. I still didn't really know what to expect, and I started playing scenes from scary movies in my head. I imagined sliding under the machine, which then took a mind of its own and trapped me. Unable to escape, I screamed for help. Just as my mind drifted off, there was a gentle knock at the door.

      The doctor introduced himself, said it would be a rather quick procedure, and they would send the results to my specialist. They gave the option to wait for the CD after imaging was complete. He explained that the machine I was staring at was to take X-Rays of my uterus and instructed me to lie down flat on my back and do not move. He then inserted a special dye into my uterus using a thin catheter. As he inserted the fluid I felt this sensation, sort of like a pinch. It didn't hurt too much but it was definitely uncomfortable. This allows him to capture pictures as the dye travels through my uterus and fallopian tubes. If there were any blockage, the next step would be a laparoscopy. The doctor lowered the machine as far down as it would go leaving it directly on top of me. He repeated that I couldn't move, as he disappeared behind the wall to take pictures of my uterus. It wasn't long before he was done getting what he needed. Once the images were ready, I was instructed to take them back to my fertility specialist who would explain everything to me.

"Did everything look normal?" I asked, hoping to get a hint of what the images told.

"Your doctor will explain everything," He repeated. As I walked out of the office, I wondered if he saw something serious. Was he afraid to tell me? Or was this just protocol? I held onto the mysterious CD for an entire day before I met with my fertility specialist again.

The next day my doctor put the CD into the computer and began downloading the images. He was quiet as he looked intensely at the images, and I wondered how he could even tell what he was looking at. To me it was just white shadows with some specs here and there. He looked up from the computer.

"I'm going to recommend a laparoscopy," he said. Apparently, there was an abnormality that showed in the x-rays. "There is scar tissue on one of your fallopian tubes, which can cause blockage." I didn't really understand what I was being told, but it sounded extremely scary. He explained that the scar tissue could be endometriosis, or perhaps from a previously untreated infection. I felt embarrassed. Ashamed. How could something like this get passed me? I saw my doctors on a regular basis and got tested every year. My test results always came back negative. It was confusing to me. When did this happen? How long ago was it? Why did I not see the signs? The specialist was kind and assured me that it happens more often than I would think. But it didn't comfort me to think about how often it happened to others, and I found myself in tears that it happened to me.

He went on to explain the potential causes for the blockage in my fallopian tubes, and that there was a possibility I would encounter difficulties conceiving through IUI. The laparoscopy would confirm if I could even move forward with the intrauterine insemination or if I would have to take other options into consideration.

It can be dreadful realizing there is something wrong with your body and you cannot control it. I began to feel as though I had disappointed myself. It was clear this blockage I had in my fallopian tubes could very much be the reason I had not been able to conceive prior to this moment. I struggled as I tried to stay positive and continue to maintain my hope, while feeling such an immense disappointment. How could I remain positive when all I wanted to do was to have a precious little baby and the odds are mounted against me before even beginning the process? I had to look at the facts and come to a realization that this may be a bit more challenging than I had thought. At the same time, I wouldn't give up. I knew what I wanted and what the end goal was. I knew I was not the type of person to give up hope. I also knew that if I remained strong and followed through, I would get more concrete answers. I am not the type of person to get a bit of bad news and give up. I am a fighter. Being stubborn also helps at times like this. So instead of becoming discouraged, I started doing research on the laparoscopy. I wanted to know what I was getting myself into before I got to the doctor's office. Although my fertility specialist explained what the procedure was and that he would be the one to perform it, I knew that doing some research would make me feel more confident in going into procedure. I spent nights reading different websites and articles, until I felt prepared. I sat in the bed until the early hours of the morning, as my wife slept soundly beside me. I learned that the surgery was roughly an hour long and recovery should be about three weeks. I learned what I needed to and kept praying.

October 2012

Next time anyone tells you your recovery from surgery will be minimal don't believe it. Nope... Not only did it take nearly an hour for me to get up three flights of stairs, I am in so much pain! "Just a bit sore" my ass...I refuse to take these pain meds and I will not sit here crying...
Okay maybe I will cry just a little...
You know what though? I am a fighter! I might be a bit stubborn but still a fighter nonetheless. I will tell you one thing, I have discovered that going under is by far one of the scariest things I have ever done. I pray I never have to do that again. Now excuse me while I eat the rest of these graham crackers like a champ!

Going in for the outpatient procedure had my nerves going through all sorts of twists and turns. I felt as though my stomach was doing flips. I even began to feel nauseous. I have never had a surgery before. I have never broken any bones, been to the emergency room as an adult, or even had so much a few cuts scrapes and bruises. I had never been under anesthesia. I was completely terrified.

Denise sat by my side as the nurses prepped me for the procedure. "Everything is going to be alright," she kept reminding me. "You are incredibly strong. You got this." I couldn't have been more thankful for her than I was at that very moment. Although I was scared to move forward with this procedure, I knew it had to be done, so I put my big girl pants on and signed the paperwork.

The wait seemed like forever, but then finally they came to take me into the operating room. There was a metal table right in the middle of the room. The room was white and bright and completely sterile, exactly the way you see it on television. There were several nurses and a couple of doctors talking amongst themselves. My nerves were getting the best of me.

They moved me onto the table and began explaining what

would happen during the procedure. The anesthesiologist came over and introduced himself. He explained what he was doing and how I would feel. Then he told me he will count to 20 and I would fall asleep. He explained how I might feel when I woke up and that my doctor would be there once the procedure was over. He began counting, "One…two…three…four…five…"

The next thing I knew, there were machines beeping and people talking in what seemed to be a far distance. I opened my eyes but couldn't see much at first. A few moments slipped by and I started to piece together where I was and what was going on. I was in post-op. Thankful that I woke up with everything intact, I tried to get up from the bed. I did not succeed. I still felt groggy and a bit dizzy from the anesthesia, and my belly was in intense pain. It felt very sore. Denise joked about snagging some extra graham crackers. She knew how much I loved those. The doctor came in to tell me the procedure was successful; he was able to remove most of the scar tissue and was quite happy with the results. We would discuss it in greater detail at our follow up appointment back at his office.

"You will experience post-op pain for a few weeks," he warned, and gave me a prescription for the pain.

In order for me to be released, I had to walk to the bathroom unassisted, urinate, and then walk back on my own. *No problem,* I thought to myself. I will be out of here in no time. As I tried again to get up from the bed, I quickly realized I would be there a lot longer than anticipated. So instead of letting it wound my ego, I sat there and enjoyed my apple juice and graham crackers.

Finally I was able to get out of bed. My wife accompanied me to the bathroom in case I needed assistance. As I sat on the toilet, I began feeling really dizzy as if I was going to pass out. I whispered to my wife to help me get up.

"Don't you dare call the nurse," I warned her. "Or I'll kick your butt! I am getting out of this place!" As she helped me up, I almost lost my balance but quickly straightened up as one of the nurses opened the door to check on me. I put on a brave face and nodded that I was okay. At that point, I was willing to say anything that would get me home.

Going home that day was a challenge. I had to climb three

flights of stairs. That's when I realized how much work my core does on a daily basis. Going through this procedure made me appreciate my body in a way I never had. Something so simple as going up some steps – putting one foot in front of the other – was hindered not because of an injury to my legs, but because of an abdominal surgery. Muscles in my body that I never even saw did powerful work of keeping me moving. It took a long time to get up the stairs and Denise was helping me get through it one step at a time. She cheered me on, saying, "Great job, Chris! You can do this." But the pain increased with every step I took. My energy was decreasing and I felt like a total mess. I shot her a look to shut up - the type of look that can send someone running.

After a few days we went back to the fertility specialist's office and spoke about the results of the procedure. During this time, I discovered that I was still a candidate for the IUI procedure. However, my chances of getting pregnant using this method would be lessened due to me having the some scar tissue left in the right fallopian tube. He explained that although most of the scar tissue was removed, he was not able to completely remove the scar tissue without it damaging the fallopian tube. The good news was that I did still have the left tube, which was completely clear and ready to go. The specialist began explaining that for some couples it can take years to conceive. He was very clear on what my expectations should be. Nothing was going to stop me. I wanted a baby and I was going to give this procedure a shot.

Its Baby-Making Time!

November 2012

Who would've thought that running through Target like two kids to purchase some ovulation kits would be this much fun! I didn't even care that people were staring. We were laughing and joking and playing around. I felt like a kid again...

It was just Denise and me, this is our time and my story.

I must admit, tonight was the happiest night I have had in a few months. I have been so overwhelmed and stressed out. I needed this. And we have the video to prove it! It is baby-making time! Let's do this!

When we left the doctor's office, we went straight to the Target in our local shopping center to purchase a couple of ovulation test kits. Who knew there would be so many options to choose from?! The store places the pregnancy test kits, ovulation test kits and condoms all in the same isle. For some reason we found it comical and it was like watching two full-grown kids playing in a candy shop. There were so many different brands of ovulation kits and pregnancy tests we couldn't keep up! "Here are some ovulation test kits so you can plan your pregnancy, right next to the pregnancy tests just to confirm and if you decide to back out at the last minute… BOOM! Here are some condoms as well." Denise jokingly said as she grabbed all three boxes. We had to make light of the situation. We each performed our own version of what advertising commercials would sound like in that isle. People passed by and gave us weird looks, which made it even funnier. There is even a video of it that we watch from time to time. It was an exciting time for us. After playing around in the store, we purchased what we needed to and went home to get ready for the morning.

I am not a morning person. So waking up at 5am every morning waiting to get a smiley face on the ovulation kit was the worst. On top of drinking a couple of bottles of water first thing in the morning to make myself urinate on the ovulation test kit, we also had to measure my temperature along with blood work from the doctor to check hormone levels. We had a chart to help us keep track of everything we did in the morning. Not to mention going to the doctors first thing in the morning for an ultrasound to make sure I had follicles that were maturing properly. After days of patiently waiting I finally got a smiley face! I called the fertility office bright and early and they wanted me to go in for the first insemination. Since lived right across the street, we got there in minutes. I was going through so many emotions at the same time. I was nervous yet excited, scared and curious. I shook my leg uncontrollably while I was waiting for the doctor to call me in, unable to sit still. I barely heard anything around me. I remember looking up at the television to watch the news but couldn't focus on what they were saying. Finally the door opened and they called my name.

  Denise and I walked into the room hand in hand. Once I was undressed from the waist down, the specialist came back into the room, asked me to put my feet on the stir ups and he began the process. It is sort of like getting a pap smear done. They use a speculum and then insert a catheter and insert the specimen into the catheter. Once all of the sperm is inserted, they remove the catheter and then the speculum. The entire process in itself takes about 10 minutes. The insemination portion is very brief and takes less than a minute. It didn't hurt at all, although they warned me that I might feel some cramping and even experience light spotting afterwards. Once the doctor has completed the insemination, he asked me to remain lying down for another 10 minutes before getting dressed. Of course, while we were waiting Denise was taking pictures and videos to capture the moment. I said a prayer to myself before getting up. "Dear God, I pray that this process works for me. I ask that you please bring me a healthy baby that I can love unconditionally. In your name I pray, Amen." I was hopeful.

After the 10 minutes were up, I got dressed and headed for the nurse's station. When setting up the follow up appointment the nurse went over what I should expect and when to call if necessary. The nurse explained there would be a waiting period of exactly two weeks to begin testing my HCG levels. HCG is the human chorionic gonadotropin level, which measures your hormone levels. This is also known as Beta testing. Typically these numbers are supposed to increase as you move further into pregnancy.

The Wait

December 5, 2012

This day is one for the books! I did it we did it! I got inseminated! I have to say I probably lost a few calories with how much my nervous leg was shaking all day long!

The process was so much quicker than I anticipated. It was all over in one two three. I finally got to see the specimen. Not to mention the fact that we spent $1100.00 on each vial of specimen and my pinky finger was longer than that vial.

I am definitely in the wrong business!

It's okay though! I am full of joy and excitement and nothing can take this moment away.

December 11, 2012

Do you really think I can wait for two whole weeks? Ha ha ha ... NO. I couldn't help it!!! I caved. I bought a couple of pregnancy tests. I cannot wait to get home!

Okay, maybe I should wait like the nurse told me to... Staring at this box of pregnancy tests is like holding a lollipop up to a toddler's face. There is only so much time that will pass before I start kicking and screaming, too! I need to know!

Negative... yup, I should have waited.

December 19, 2012

Well... it's a no go for me. The doctor confirmed what the pregnancy tests were saying. I was not pregnant. This was to be expected right? Not by me. I have to admit I am feeling some type of way right now. Should I just give up? I don't know how long I can continue on month after month going through this heartache. It really hurts... I had a lot of hope.

My cycle should be coming back around in about a week or so... Do I have it in me for another try?

I have a lot to think about. Now if only I can get these tears to stop flowing.

January 2, 2013

After listening to the Pastor preaching about things happening immediately, I decided to give the fertility doctor a second try at an IUI. Yesterday was my first positive LH Surge and today is day 16 of my cycle. The doctor this time took his time was very careful and positive. This time as I stare at the clock I can hear my wife's voice in the background. Tick...tick...tick... "Lord, please bless me with my little angel. I am praying for a healthy full-term pregnancy and I am praying for a healthy little boy or girl. In your name I pray, Amen.

January 12, 2013
Fourteen days?! Who knew waiting 14 days would be so challenging? I am sitting here on the toilet contemplating, should I do it? My wife is in the room sleeping and I have to wait four more days to find out for sure. Ah what they heck... Negative...
Should I take this as a sign? I do not feel good about this at all. Maybe I should have waited.
Don't cry... Please don't cry...

Do you really think I was able to wait for two weeks? 14 days? Absolutely not! All day, everyday all I could focus on is being pregnant. I kept thinking I could be pregnant right now. This thought literally crossed my mind at least every 10 to 15 minutes. I kept a pregnancy test in the bathroom for a few days and stared at it every time I went into the bathroom. I only lasted about four or five days before I couldn't take the suspense any longer. Sitting anxiously waiting for the test to tell me if I were pregnant, I felt my heart racing. Negative… okay so maybe I should have waited like the nurse explained. Or maybe I should just try again the next day; after all, the box that I purchased came with two pregnancy tests. But the pregnancy test the next morning came out negative as well. This went on for another couple of days before I decided to listen to the nurse and wait the remainder of the time. On day fourteen I had to go in to check my HCG level and give them a urine sample and both confirmed that I was not pregnant. My heart sank as the fertility specialist explained that this is to be expected especially with what they found in the laparoscopy. So now what?

The doctor explained to me that I would have to wait until my next menstrual cycle and we do it all over again. I left the office that day in tears. I was completely heart broken. I know I had to keep the faith and understand that things take time but I didn't want to. I didn't want to wait. I didn't want to be disappointed again. I was upset with myself but I knew I had to keep pushing through this.

A few weeks later, I had the computer on and I was streaming online to the church service going on that Sunday morning. The pastor was preaching about things not happening immediately and what happens when they do. He preached, "We are always rushing for things to happen, always complaining that things do not go our way. Not everything is meant to happen when you want it to happen. We are living in God's world and things are meant to happen when He says so. We expect our children to be patient but we tend to forget that we are children as well. We are God's children and He wants us to be patient! Wait for your blessings! Don't you know the best things come to those who wait?" It was a reminder to me that I cannot have control over everything and I needed to allow my body the chance to do what it is meant to do. I decided at that moment I would give IUI another shot. I waited for the happy face on the ovulation test to confirm my LH surge. LH stands for luteinizing hormone and it detects ovulation. One day 16 of my cycle I got a happy face and called the fertility office immediately. Normally I would be instructed to come into the office the same day but today was different. The doctor said he wanted me to come in the following morning instead of that morning. He said he wanted me to wait one more day. So I did…

The next morning I was back at the doctor's office waiting for my next insemination. Once I got into the room I undressed from the waist down, laid on the bed and waited for the doctor to come into the office. He made us verify the specimen number. He was a different doctor from the first time. After explaining the process, he carefully inserted the speculum then the catheter and slowly began inserting the sperm. He stopped every few seconds and looked at his watch. It was almost as though he was timing the injection of the sperm into the catheter. It seemed like forever as he completed the process and removed the catheter then the speculum and told me to lie down for about 10 minutes and then I was free to go. When he left the room he turned and said "Good luck to you." I could hear my Denise's voice as though it was off in the distance. I could also hear the hands on the clock moving as I closed my eyes and said, "Lord, please bless me with my little angel. I am asking you for a healthy full-term pregnancy and a healthy little boy or girl that I can love unconditionally, in your name I pray. Amen". The next 10 minutes we sat together and there were no pictures or videos to capture anything this time. We just sat together in complete silence.

Once the ten minutes were up, we walked to the nurse's station and set up the next follow up appointment. Although we lived just across the street, there was a huge intersection dividing a four way street so we always drove to and from the office. Denise grabbed my hand and asked if I was okay. I nodded and we spent the rest of the ride in silence. I went to work as usual, only today I didn't think about the procedure that took place that morning. As I drove to work, I turned the radio off and I just sat in the car in silence. I could feel the tears building up in my eyes but I kept wiping them away before they streamed down my cheeks. I was trying to remain strong and hopeful but I couldn't help being scared that I may be let down again. A couple of days went by and I started thinking of being pregnant again. The excitement was building and I couldn't take it anymore. I fought with myself and even left my debit card home just so that I wouldn't purchase any pregnancy tests while I was out.

A few days later, I caved and purchased a box of pregnancy tests. Did you really expect for me to wait 14 entire days all over again? I waited ten days and believe me it was nerve wrecking! Who knew waiting 14 days would be so challenging! When I got home, I went straight into the bathroom and locked the door. I sat on the toilet for a while contemplating my next move. After much deliberation, and a raging debate in my mind, I decided not to do it. I put the box underneath the sink and left the bathroom. I thought to myself, *it's only four more days.* In four days, I would go to the doctor and have my blood test, and I would know for sure.

Later on that evening Denise was sleeping and I grew bored. She always falls asleep first. I went into the bathroom to brush my teeth and get ready for bed. All of a sudden, it was as though the little sticks were calling out to me, begging me to open them up and test them out already. I grabbed the box that held my destiny. I sat on the toilet and waited. I saw something in the screen of the pregnancy test and I was so nervous that I didn't check it right away. I almost threw it out because I was so afraid to see what it would say. I stared at the words 'not pregnant' for what seemed to be a long time. Long enough for my legs to go numb from sitting on the toilet for too long.

Should I take this as a sign? I do not feel good about this at all. Why would it not be positive? What have I done? Is this some sort of bad karma? Maybe I should have just waited like they told me. I never listen. My mom used to tell me how stubborn I was. I closed my eyes took a deep breathe and whispered to myself, "don't cry… please don't cry."

Nevertheless, tears filled my eyes as I went to bed. I was hurt and didn't understand what was going on with my body. I stayed up most of the night, staring at the wall. In the morning, I didn't say anything to Denise because I knew she would remind me that I was supposed to wait and this is what happens when I don't listen. I didn't want to hear it, so I kept it to myself. A few more days went by and I realized I had another pregnancy test left over from the box I had purchased a few days back. Very tempted, I fought with myself to stay out of the bathroom. I even held my urine in longer than I should have to simply avoid being tempted to take the pregnancy test.

    I couldn't sleep that night. I was coming up on day 14 – the day of the blood test. Unable to stay in bed, I paced the living room back and forth. I thought to myself, what if the IUI didn't work for the second time? I remembered how heartbroken I was the first time around. What if I am pregnant right now? Something inside of me kept urging me towards the bathroom to take the final test. I just needed to know! I had already spent the night crying – the test results wouldn't change that. I convinced myself. Sitting there nervously awaiting the test results, my mind began to drift. I imagined myself sitting there as I watched my little munchkin running around the house. I could almost hear the most angelic little voice calling for me. Just as I began to get lost in my thoughts, a message came up on the screen. I sat there for a moment staring at the pregnancy test. "Pregnant." *I am pregnant!* I felt a rush flowing through my body and I burst out of the bathroom and ran into the bedroom shouting to Denise " I'm pregnant! I'm pregnant!" It was 1:30 in the morning and I startled her awake, scaring her as I jumped on the bed. Groggy, she began to understand what I was saying, and we sat together on the bed, crying with happiness.

January 17, 2013

Today I find myself so excited that I even woke up before the alarm went off! Mark this one down in history. On my way to the doctor's office, I cannot help myself but to smile freakishly the whole entire way there (literally). It is six in the morning! Who could possibly be this happy? Me! I am pregnant! So I had my first blood test today and of course the results confirmed what I already knew... I can barely contain myself and I just want to scream it out to the world! OH! Nothing can take this joy I am feeling.

The next morning, before the alarm went off, I awoke with a feeling of excitement. I even woke up before the alarm went off in spite of me not getting much sleep during the evening. I was elated! You know that feeling you get the night before going on a vacation, or even as a teenager knowing you were going to Six Flags or Disney

World the next day? That is how I felt! The anticipation filled every space on my skin, every bone inside my body. I smiled the entire way to the doctor's office. If you had seen me, you might have wondered out loud, "It is six o'clock in the morning, who could possibly be this happy?"

And to that, I would have shouted, "I am!"

"Why?" you might then ask.

"Because I am pregnant!" I would scream to you and the world!

Once I got to the office, the nurse did the first blood test and the results confirmed that I was pregnant. My HCG levels had to be at least 50 to confirm pregnancy, and they were at 62! Good job uterus! I could barely contain my joy -nothing in the world could take this feeling away. I felt relieved to know that I deserved this. I was good enough to be a mother. I felt like the luckiest woman in the world because someone up there in the great unknown knew I would be a great mother and they chose me for this little being that is growing inside of my belly.

The First Trimester

January 19, 2013

Today is Saturday and I cannot think of anything besides this tiny little baby growing inside of me. I have downloaded a bunch of apps and books to my devices. Who knew there was so much information to learn? Right now my little peanut is working hard developing the heart, lungs, stomach and other bodily systems. Grow baby grow! Mommy is so proud of you!

With the confirmation of my pregnancy, I began researching websites on what to expect throughout the pregnancy. I downloaded apps such as Oh Baby! and What to Expect When Expecting. They have fun facts about each week of pregnancy and how big the baby would be. I also purchased a small library of books. I was a first-time mom to be and I immediately became hooked on the whole baby hype. Who knew there was so much information to learn? One website told me that my little peanut was right now working hard to develop the heart, lungs, stomach, and other bodily systems. *Grow baby grow! Mommy is so proud of you!* I whispered to my womb.

January 21, 2013
As tired as I am, I am up at six in the morning again for round two of beta testing. I was excited with the results. That's right baby, keep on growing! Mommy is out here cheering you on!
Although I am now on my way to work, I am completely exhausted and it is only seven in the morning. All I want to do is jump in my bed and go right back to sleep. Not to mention my constant trips to the porcelain throne...
I am going through so many changes from tender breasts to wacky cravings but I am totally in love with it all...

A couple of days after my first blood test; I was scheduled for my round two of beta testing. At 6AM, I was up and heading to the fertility specialist's office. My HCG levels were at 323! They more than tripled in just a few days. I am so proud of my little baby! All I really wanted to do was go back to bed and fall asleep, but I couldn't – I had to go to work. I soon started to notice that my body was already going through so many changes. I was beginning to use the bathroom more frequently, my breasts were sensitive and I was constantly tired. I refused to complain because I felt I had no right to. This is what I had been yearning for and I could only be thankful for this entire experience.

January 22, 2013

So I am at work today walking around, greeting customers, working hard and the urge comes. So I take a break and head to my favorite room of all time these days... To my surprise, my worst fear. Right now I can't think straight, my hands are shaking and my eyes are quickly becoming swollen from holding my tears in. Squeezing my eyes shut, I hold my stomach and pray. "Lord I know you would not give me this miracle only to take it away. Help me."

At work the day after my second beta test, I felt an extra sense of excitement that I had a tiny little secret growing inside of me. It would have seemed to everyone else business as usual as I greeted clients and mingled with coworkers. But I had the most exciting secret. Could they tell by my smile? Did they notice the amount of times I headed to the bathroom? I wondered as I went to the bathroom for the fifth time that morning. And then to my surprise, I realized my worst fear was happening right before my eyes. I saw blood. At that moment I sat there confused and scared. I couldn't even think straight. A thousand thoughts flew through my mind, and none settled. My eyes were swelling up quickly as I tried to fight back tears. I squeezed my eyes shut, I held my belly and prayed. *Lord, please let my baby be okay, I ask that you keep my munchkin healthy and safe. Amen.* I knew I would not be given this wonderful miracle just to have it snatched right from me. I mean that would be horrible right? It just didn't make sense. I called the doctor in a panic and explained what was going on. The nurse instructed me to stay calm and wait until tomorrow. I tried my hardest to get through the day, telling myself that if they thought it was an emergency, they would have called me in right away. That night, I fell asleep as early as possible. I had my final round of beta testing early in the morning and I would find out exactly what was going on inside of me.

  The next morning, I woke up before the alarm went off and I lay in bed staring up at the ceiling. I was nervous and afraid of what may happen next. I allowed my nerves to get the best of me. It is natural for a pregnant woman to be edge about what could happen and you forget to stay in the present moment. But in this case, there had been blood. I waited anxiously to get the results of the third beta test.

January 23, 2013

Well, all is well that ends well. Today was my final round of beta testing. HCG levels are at 759. My numbers are more than doubling and Dr. Baby Maker says that I am in a great position. Ahhhhhh I am so relieved. I spoke to the nurse about the bleeding in which she responded, "brown blood is old blood." So I let it go. My baby is doing an awesome job! Grow baby grow! Although the baby is so very tiny at this point, I am elated that this little angel is mine all mine.

"759," my doctor announced. My little munchkin was growing perfectly. The doctor said my numbers had more than doubled, which was a great thing. I breathed a sigh a relief and listened as he continued to explain that brown blood is old blood and my body was adjusting to being pregnant. Although the baby was so tiny at this point, I was elated that this little angel was all mine, at least for now. For the next few days, I laid low. I was trying to be careful, to be safe. I realized the more I worried about something happening, the less I got to enjoy the experience. I had to learn to practice mindfulness and just be grateful to be able to bear a child. I understood that so many women go through years of hurt and disappointment, unable to conceive as quickly as I did. I was lucky.

Or maybe not so lucky… Nearly 13 days later, I began to spot again. Only this time, the blood was deep red and it was more than the first time. I frantically called the doctor who checked me out right away.

"The baby looks good," he said. "It could be stress from work." He placed me on immediate bed rest and explained that pushing myself can be draining which in turn causes stress. That much stress isn't particularly good for a woman who is still in her first trimester. It is the most critical stage in any pregnancy. I stayed up all night that evening worrying. Although the doctor assured me the baby was fine, it was going to be difficult for me to be on bed rest for the new few days. I was so used to being up and active throughout the day and now I cannot do anything.

Going to the bathroom caused much anxiety as I braced myself each time for more blood. It was to a point where my body would shake knowing I had to go. The following day seemed to be more of a relief as the spotting had come and gone. My little munchkin was certainly giving me a run for my money.

I didn't have many symptoms besides feeling tired and experiencing frequent trips to the bathroom. I also began craving sweets. I tried not to feed into the cravings and attempted to satisfy them with fruit.

February 7, 2013
Well they say you can only go in one direction after hitting rock bottom and that is up! Today I learned that despite the hurt my heart has endured from this pregnancy, my baby is growing perfectly. I had the pleasure of hearing the baby's heartbeat for the first time today! I am so addicted to that sound. To see my wife's face light up the way it did made me happy to bring someone else as much joy as this baby is bringing me.

During my next appointment, I was given a sweet surprise. I heard the baby's heartbeat for the first time: 152 beats per minute (BPM). It was absolutely the best sound in the entire world to me, and I felt myself becoming addicted to the thumping. It was official: I was in love. I was able to record the heartbeat on my cell phone, and I must have listened to it at least 30 times that day alone. My heart raced every time I heart it. It was the sweetest sound. I could not believe how much joy this little munchkin was bringing me.

On February 14, Valentine's Day, I found myself spotting yet again. This time the spotting was light pink and it wasn't as much as the last time, but it was there and noticeable. It was hard to understand what could be happening and all I kept thinking about was the worst. This was now the third time I had experienced bleeding and I didn't know how to react. Part of me wanted to remain calm while the other part wanted to break down into tears and hide away. I needed to know what was happening inside of my body and why it was reacting this way to the pregnancy. I think any mother to be would understand how scared and worried I became. I knew I was being tested. They say pregnancy brings on these raging hormones that cause your moods to change from one minute to the next but nobody ever prepares you for these situations. It was completely challenging. I wanted nothing more than to be able to kiss those tiny little hands and tiny little feet in just seven more months. I was not giving up on my baby and I prayed this little being didn't give up on me.

February 15, 2013

I am here at the doctor's office waiting patiently, very patiently. I am just wondering why is it that when you set an appointment for a specific time, you almost never see the doctor at that time! I have an emergency! What is going on? I need an explanation! Now!! So much for me being patient. I am exploding on the inside... "Christina Rios." *Sigh* Finally... The doctor checks me and finds that it is all good. According to what the doctor can see, both the baby and myself are both doing fine and the baby is growing perfectly. Now I can go home and relax.

At the doctor's office the next morning, I failed at my attempt to wait patiently. I paced back and forth and asked the receptionist about two or three times if the wait would be much longer. I only wanted to know if my baby was doing fine. I needed an explanation as to what was going on inside of my body. I wondered to myself what was taking them so long to call me. You would think if you show up early for an appointment you scheduled at a specific time, they would be ready! Each minute that passed felt like an eternity. "I have an emergency!" I wanted to scream. Seconds away from jumping out of my seat yet again and expressing my anger with the poor receptionist, one of the nurses opened the door and called my name. It was almost as if the receptionist knew what was coming her way because as I walked past her desk she smiled and quickly turned the other way. As the doctor was checking the baby out, he started to explain what implantation is. It is when the embryo adheres to the wall of the uterus. It happens in the beginning of pregnancy and one in every three women are likely to experience actual bleeding from this process. He also explained to me that bleeding this time could simply be me approaching what would have been my next menstrual cycle. It is just my body adjusting to being pregnant. According to the doctor I was healthy and my baby was growing perfectly. Now that I had a better understanding of what was happening, I could go home and relax. I decided to celebrate this victory with a nice long nap.

The changes you go through as a woman when a child is involved are amazing. Your body is not the only thing that changes. Yes, we go through the motions of being pregnant and the tender breasts, cravings, and constantly being tired, but your mind also changes. The way you think, act, and speak changes. You begin to express love in a different way. You suddenly begin to appreciate life more. On February 25, the best thing happened. I was sitting on the couch and it was exactly 2:58PM. I felt the baby move for the first time! It felt weird; I didn't know what it was but then a few minutes later after paying close attention to my body it happened again. It felt sort of like a tickling sensation. I had the biggest smile on my face and waited for it to happen again but after some time passed, I did not feel it again. I pulled out my phone and began searching the web for other moms who has experienced this so early on. To my surprise there were plenty of mothers who were lucky enough to experience early movements. It is also known as 'quickening'. The smile refused to dissipate. It had easily become the best day of my life yet. I was so excited for what would come next.

Time was quickly passing me by and before I knew it my wife's birthday was approaching. I felt bad taking the spotlight off of her but it was all for a very good reason. On the day of Denise's birthday, we had another doctor's appointment. This is a special one because the baby would now be big enough to get an ultrasound of the face! I explained the tickling sensation to the doctor and they did confirm that it could very well have been the baby moving. He explained most mothers do not feel movement until later on while others are lucky to feel it earlier. I felt proud. Not because I was learning so much and getting better at handling situations as they come in the pregnancy but because I realized these situations were preparing me to be strong enough to be a great mother. To ice the cake, I also had the opportunity to hear the baby's heartbeat again! This time it was stronger and much louder than the last. I was beginning to love these appointments. I am measured 11 weeks and three days pregnant. My estimated due date was September 24th. In just a couple more weeks I would be in my second trimester and my chances of the big bad M-word will drastically decrease. I would be out of the red zone and would be able to enjoy this pregnancy even more.

March 10, 2013

As I hold my growing belly, I imagine how big my baby is getting. He or she is already stealing my heart. I smile inside every time he or she moves. I love being tickled from the inside. There is nothing more magical. I must take a moment to thank the Lord that my pregnancy has been mild. I am one of the lucky ones, as I have not had one single day of morning sickness. My little jumping bean does like to move around at night, so I do not get much sleep. Something tells me it will all be worth it in the end.

    I often found myself thinking about how the pregnancy started off. It was a rocky beginning. I had experienced mood swings from almost the very start. I don't know where they come from. One minute I was completely fine and then next thing I knew any little thing would set me off. However, it hadn't all been bad. For one thing, I had not endured one single day of morning sickness. I hadn't come across one single thing that made me nauseous. Soon I would be in my second trimester and I could finally fully enjoy being pregnant.

March 13, 2013

Well, well, well... I am pleased to announce that I am almost in my second trimester! I still feel the same but my belly is beginning to become a hard. Sometimes I wish there were a special machine that pregnant women can take home to see their little babies in the womb doing whatever it is they do. At the same time, I am afraid that if such a thing where possible, we would not get a single thing done! All I want is for my baby to be here so I can stare into his or her eyes and cuddle until baby falls fast asleep on my chest.

March 28, 2013

Who said pregnancy was supposed to be perfect? Today has not been a good day for me at all! I have been having mood swings like you wouldn't believe! Why did I come to work today? I feel like I am the only one working! My lunch is not hot enough, I have a headache and I just want to scream! I am not kidding... if one more person asks me to use the... Hmmm... it's almost as though this baby knows when I am about to explode into tears. Just when I feel as though I've had enough, my baby reminds me of my purpose. Now I will go grab a chocolate bar and indulge in its yummy goodness.

The Second Trimester

March 30, 2013

I have had such a long week. All I really want to do is rest. I feel so drained. I have made up my mind today is a lazy day.
"Babe c'mon get dressed, I want to take you out for lunch."
Sighs And there goes the big "DO NOT DISTURB" sign that hung above my head all morning.
Have any of you other pregnant women out there just want to cry because you don't want to do anything? That is how I am feeling right now!

In the car I check my usual applications and learn that this month baby may be sucking his or her thumbs, yawning and maybe even stretching! Keep growing for mommy baby! I love you!

Hello second trimester! With the advent of the second trimester, my chances for a miscarriage have now significantly decreased and I felt that I could finally breathe! I had heard so many stories about other mothers not making it this far into their pregnancies, and I realized that being pregnant was such a beautiful gift. I would never take it for granted, knowing it could be taken away at any given moment and for any reason. I had no choice but to be grateful. Being in a same sex marriage has made the process that much more difficult with the testing, the waiting, the timing of blood work, medical procedures and evaluations as well as the patience required to get through all of it. I was truly thankful for being able to carry a child of my very own. So many people don't realize what we go through or what it feels like to be someone who wants a child so very bad but have the odds stacked against you. With April quickly approaching, I thought about the people who joke around about being pregnant for April Fools' Day. I had never taken it lightly to be pregnant nor did I appreciate the jokes of people pretending to be pregnant.

I am learning to appreciate life, not that I didn't before, but I believe that sometimes it just takes something like this whole process to make you realize that life shouldn't be wasted away doing things that will not matter in the end. Making it this far into pregnancy changed me. Knowing that in approximately 5 months I would be a mother changed the way I think, but also the way I carried myself, and the way I love. I cannot help this change. I embrace it.

In the second trimester, I was constantly tired. Sometimes I just wanted to cry because I wanted to do nothing at all. But it was fun to learn about what my little peanut could be doing inside of my womb. Checking my usual applications on my phone I learned that the baby could be sucking his or her thumbs, yawning, and even stretching! During this time in my pregnancy my baby now had eyelids, eyebrows, nails and even hair! I wondered if my baby would have a lot of hair. Will he or she have my smile and my eyes? These are things that I looked forward to finding out. I did know one thing for certain: at this stage in my pregnancy, the genitals were fully developed so I would soon be able to find out the sex of my little munchkin. I wished I had a remote control that could fast forward time…

I was not ready to share this news with the world just yet but I want those closest to us to know. The first people I told were my parents and siblings. I was sitting by the computer and had my sonogram pictures so I decided to video chat with them so I could also see their reactions. Surely, they would have to be at least half as excited as I was! I remember it being a little less exciting than what I imagined it would be. They were all nonchalant about seeing the sonogram picture. It did hurt just a little, but I was too happy to allow anything to take away from my happiness and excitement. Knowing that I am now in my fourth month and feeling how hard my belly was starting to become was happiness in and of itself.

At 17 weeks and three days into my pregnancy, I laid down on the medical table for my second trimester screening. I could not take my eyes off of the screen. I didn't even care that the gel for the sonogram was cold. I only wanted to know how my baby was doing. I learned that baby was growing right on track and measurements looked great. It was so weird that the baby was moving around inside of me, and I could actually see it happening on the screen. Then the nurse asked us the magical question, "Would you like to know the sex of your baby?" I think in that moment, we both just shook our heads yes and waited for the nurse to answer us. Those few moments felt like an eternity, before the nurse announced we were having a boy!

Denise was so excited that she jumped up. In that exact moment, watching her grab her blue Yankee fitted cap and jumping in the air I realized, this was the happiest I had seen her yet. I was already elated just to be having a healthy baby, and now even more so, knowing it would be a boy that I would watch grow up to become a wholesome young man. But there was something uniquely special in that moment of witnessing my wife in such a state of pure joy. Even looking back and reliving this moment I am sitting here smiling because it is the little things like this in life that are most important. This is what life is made up of, a million little things. These moments of happiness is what keeps everything together when we feel our world can fall apart.

April 23, 2013
So the wife and I were sitting down relaxing when we realize a one-bedroom apartment is not big enough for the new baby. We both grew up in two totally different environments. She has always had her own bedroom and I have always had to share

mine. During our conversation we begin discussing how we want to raise our son and all of the things we want to do for him. Going into my fifth month of pregnancy, I begin to wonder how in the world am I going to manage pregnancy, moving into a new place and a full time very demanding job?
Let the stress begin...

As the pregnancy progressed, Denise and I came to realize that our cozy one bedroom apartment wasn't going to be big enough for our growing family. We only had five months to find a place big enough for the three of us. It seemed like enough time, but with us both working full time jobs it really wasn't that easy to visit places and decide where we wanted to move. School districts played a big part in our decision. I could feel the stress mounting. My wife would have to shoulder the majority of the burden on her own, moving the boxes out of the old place and into the new one. I knew she wouldn't let me do any of the heavy lifting.

April 28, 2013
I am not sure why but I woke up feeling worried. How are we going to be able to go look for a place big enough for the three of us in just four months? More importantly, how in the world is my wife going to do this on her own? I cannot move any heavy boxes, I already do so much during the day at work that when I

get home I am exhausted!

I look at my wife and she is focused on the computer looking for a place good enough for the family. I close my eyes...

"Lord please get us through this. I am going to put my worries in your hands, amen."

April 30, 2013

Today was a fun day. I am 19 weeks pregnant and I decided to announce my pregnancy to my co-workers. They all seemed happy for me. They are a good group of people but sometimes they have their days! Although they tend to drive me insane at times, they tried making me as comfortable as possible. I appreciated the efforts and I hope they know that but work is work no matter what. In my eyes I must stay up and hustle from the time I sign in until the time I sign out. Besides, I feel okay, not too much worn out. (I smile as I just felt the baby move again.) I love this feeling.

At 19 weeks I decided to announce my pregnancy to the people I work with. They were all happy for me and were also accommodating as much as possible. My wife and I have decided to keep the sex of the baby a secret until the baby shower. It was fun watching people guess the sex of our baby, and it was really hard keeping it a secret. I found myself pausing when I spoke about the baby so I wouldn't slip up. The more people wanted to know, the harder it was to keep it a secret!

May 5, 2013

Today is my little sister's birthday and I am excited for her. I am beginning to remember helping my mom take care of her as a baby and how special those moments were. She is now 18 years old and is going off to college. I feel proud. It gives me so much to look forward to when raising my baby. I cannot wait to watch him grow and hit milestone after milestone. Mother's Day is approaching and I am excited to celebrate my mommy-to-be day! This time next year my baby will be here and I will officially be a mother. That sure does sound nice.

Everything reminded me of the baby growing inside of me. I wondered what his future would look like. The day of my youngest sister's 18th birthday was a day filled with emotion. She would be going away to college that year and it gave me so much to look forward to for my own son. Likewise, I got to celebrate my youngest brother and godson who were both going off to high school. I was so proud of them all. I thought about watching them all grow up. At their graduations, I drifted off and imagined when it would be my son's time. As my munchkin grows, I will show him pictures and videos and talk about what he thinks about graduating. Family is everything to me and I am thankful to be able to capture these special moments not only for me but to show my son that he can do it too. I wonder what he will want to be when he grows up.

May 7, 2013
Since the wife and I are both off from work today, what could be better than going to Babies R' Us to begin our registry? I am super excited that I can finally begin shopping and picking things out for my little one! This doesn't get any better. As we arrive at our destination, we see a parking lot full of cars... I am beginning to feel lazy as I think about how far I have to walk until I see a sign in the very front of the parking lot, Reserved for Expectant Moms Only. That's me! That is me! VIP parking for the prego, that's right! I am so excited about this I just have to take a picture. Do any other first-time moms get this excited?

Things I noticed in my second trimester that I hadn't noticed before: signs that read "Reserved parking expectant moms only," during sonograms, my baby was camera-shy; a few minutes after I eat my favorite Rita's Italian Ice – strawberry starburst with coconut – my baby boy start dancing for joy; Denise and I still haven't found a new home.

May 12, 2013

Happy mommy-to-be Mother's Day! Today is a good day. My love has special plans for me and she is making me feel like a million bucks. I woke up extra early to go spend some time with my mom before the wife and I celebrate our special day. To my surprise my youngest sister and brother are whipping up a special breakfast for my mom and me. Now isn't that the sweetest thing ever? I sure do feel appreciated and special. It all just makes the anticipation of becoming a mother that much greater. In just a couple of months I will be a first-time mommy. Time to go spend the rest of this special day with my most special lady. She is taking me to my favorite restaurant for dinner! Yay!

May 15, 2013

Today I am 21 weeks and 1 day pregnant. My belly is very noticeable and I find myself taking a bunch of pictures in the mirror instead of getting ready for my doctor's appointment. During the appointment the nurse begins taking all of the measurements and is trying to get a clear picture of the baby's face. My little munchkin is giving her a run for her money though. He is twisting and turning and rolling around. Although I notice she is growing impatient, I cannot help but enjoy it because I get to watch the baby on the screen for that much longer.

May 24, 2013

Today makes 22 weeks and 3 days into my pregnancy and I felt like the day would never end! Fridays at work are always busy. My feet hurt and all I can think about is my big comfortable bed that is waiting at home for me. I get to relax this weekend and to be honest I cannot wait! It is 7PM in the evening and I am finally home. I realize I have yet to pick out an outfit for my cousin's baby shower this weekend. Not to mention we are still looking for a home to make ours before I give birth. Well, so much for resting.

To the store we go to find an outfit! First, off we go to get an icy. Strawberry starburst and coconut please! Ahhhhh... heaven in a cup.

June 1 2013

Today is my cousin's baby shower and I am happy I get to celebrate with her. She is also a first-time mommy so we often text each other about our experiences. My hair is done and I am finally ready to go. As I take my normal weekly pictures, I realize, woah... my boobs are huge! As if they weren't already big. So this is what happens when you are with child huh? It makes me wonder about what other changes I will face... One thing I have to admit though, I am wearing this cute dress and making it look good! I am in love with this growing bump and *for now the baby is mine, all mine! Baby agrees... He just kicked again.*

My cousin was an expectant first time mother as well, so we often texted each other to share our experiences throughout the pregnancy. She has her shower before I did, and it was such a wonderful and joyous day, until a family member made a snide remark as I walked past her. "So she really is pregnant," she has said. Being in a same sex marriage, my wife and I get looks of judgment all the time. You would think people would become as open minded to love and life as they are with their open mouths and closed minds yet to hear it coming from family is just disheartening. This is exactly why I hadn't told anyone else besides our immediate family and coworkers. It is sad but with growth you learn to love and take people for what they are. You learn that some things just aren't that important and you appreciate having an open mind more so for allowing you to understand that sometimes people will support you and sometimes they will not. I am learning to accept things for what they are. I am also learning to keep things and people at arm's length.

June 6, 2013

Hello 24 week and two day mark! Today my little munchkin is the size of an ear of corn... I am really excited because I can feel my baby moving around and it is just an awesome feeling to know there is a bun baking in my oven. This week on my apps they talk about growing boobs (go figure) and stretch marks and I can only laugh as I read this and think to myself "too late." Anyway, my baby boy now has developed taste buds and fingerprints are still in formation. How cool is that? I also know that my little munchkin can hear everything that is going on. I almost never share my headphones but for my baby I will share anything. Let's listen to some soft music and relax.

June 8, 2013

Today is a good day...and why is that you asked? Well because it is my day off from work and the weather is amazing! Today we are going bowling and out to eat at Joe's Crab Shack with some great friends. I am getting ready to head out and of course I am in the mirror checking myself out when it hits me. No not the growing belly or the swollen boobs, not the fact that my hair looks super cute today but yes, you have guessed it... I now have the pregnancy nose. When did my nose get so wide and so puffy? Why does this happen? How does this happen? I am devastated. It looks like I have one of those fake nose things on with the mustache attached... This better be one cute baby because he is changing my whole appearance! Although I must admit, my mommy-to-be swag is on point! Ha-ha ha-ha seriously though, I hope my nose goes back to normal.

June 9, 2013

I find myself in a bit of a good mood today. I have no clue why but it feels nice. Yesterday I kicked butt in bowling, even though my wife kept monitoring my every move. Dinner was fun too. I pretended it was my friend's birthday so they made her get up and dance while they sang happy birthday to her. As I am smiling to myself thinking about how fun yesterday was, I get excited and run to the refrigerator to see a bright shiny light surrounding my leftovers... ahhhh snack time!

To kick off my birthday month, we went to dinner and bowling with some friends. At bowling, my wife was like a spy monitoring my every move! "That ball is too heavy, don't walk too fast the floor can be slippery, do you want me to take your turn?"

No! I wanted to say. *The ball is only eight pounds and I am trying to beat you, why in the world would I let you take my turn?* I wondered if all pregnant women have to deal with this stuff or if it was just me? During church the next day, I realized that I had been thanking the higher power a lot more than I normally do. I had so much to be thankful for. I was being given the ultimate gift for the second time. I was receiving the gift of life all over again. I could not imagine a time in my life greater than it was right in that moment.

June 16, 2013

Today is Sunday and we are off to church. Any moms out there find themselves praying and thanking God (or whoever you pray to) a lot more than normal when pregnant? I guess I am because I realize I have so much more to be thankful for. Right now in this very moment God is creating a tiny human being inside of my womb just for me. He has given me the ultimate gift. I cannot imagine a time in my life greater or any more special than it is right now. As I sat down in church today, I closed my eyes and drifted away. "Lord every time my baby moves, every time I look at my growing belly, I think of you.

June 21, 2013

Hurry hurry hurry! Let me pack my bag and shower, I have to rush out of this house! It is happening! You thought I was in labor huh? Gotcha! I am not in labor, my baby is still safe inside of my belly growing bigger and bigger. Today is a very special day! My second and third babies are graduating today! My younger brother and my godson are both moving up and going off to high school. Oh my, where has the time gone? If only they knew proud I am of them. They are not so little anymore. Even the baby is excited! Settle down little one, we are going on a car ride to Brooklyn!

June 27, 2013

Happy Birthday to me! Today is Thursday so unfortunately that mean I am working today but that doesn't mean I cannot get dolled up! I love doing my hair and makeup. Although I do not have the option of what to wear at least I can enjoy some girl time in the morning, as I get ready for work. *Sighs* These shirts are getting smaller and smaller. On the bright side my baby is moving around like crazy so I am in an awesome mood right now. He must know it is his mommy's birthday. Well, as much as I would love to stay home in my jammies eating ice cream out of the carton and watching tv all day, this mommy has to make money so off to work I go...

June 28, 2013

Hello everyone! Today is yet another very special day! My younger sister is graduating from high school and going off to college! Watching her walk down the aisle is so amazing. I can't wait to tell my baby that will be him one day... Oh gosh! Sometimes being pregnant makes it hard to stop the water works but I guess I have so much to be proud of this summer. I am just trying to focus on my sister because the second I take my eyes off of her I want to scratch the skin off of my belly! Why does it itch so much? Oh well, off to lunch we go. I am starving! Do all pregnant women have an uncontrollable mind? Maybe it is just me. I don't know but my feet are killing me!

Third trimester

July 4, 2013

Hello third trimester! How elated I feel at this very moment! I have so much going on with birthdays and graduations that I did not realize how quickly time is flying by! I have survived the first and second trimester with no major complications so I am extremely thankful. I just love going for check-ups because I get to hear my little one's heartbeat. This is by far the sweetest sound in the world to me. Luckily, I recorded it so I can listen to it all the time. Is it normal to be addicted to the sound of your baby's heartbeat? Who knows what normal is anyway.

At week 28, I was now in the beginning of the third and final trimester! I could not help but to think that in just a few months I would no longer be pregnant. I listened to other moms as they shared their experiences of pregnancy with me. They all wanted to hurry up and give birth already by this time of their pregnancies. They were exhausted and worn out. Their backs hurt and their muscles ached. They just wanted it over with. But for me, it was different. I was in love with the entire journey – the good the bad and the ugly. I truly loved being pregnant, and wanted to savor every moment of it.

During the third trimester, you have to take a glucose screening. It was probably the first time I dread doing something during this pregnancy. I had to drink a whole bottle of this awful soda-like fluid drink tons of water on top of that. Then, I had to refrain from using the bathroom until the doctor gave the okay. *Is this some sort of joke?* I wondered. *Is this their way of getting you back at me for all the extra sonogram pictures and extra seconds of listening to the heartbeat that I asked for?* If so, I think it is totally unfair. This screening showed that my sugar levels are normal, but the doctor indicated that I had a bit of protein in my urine. When I asked him what this meant, he explained it could be an early sign of preeclampsia. He said it was too soon to worry about it, but that I should rest more and stress less. *Sure,* I thought. *I am working full time in a high stress environment and we still haven't found a new place to live, but okay doc.*

July 6, 2013

Well as I have said before our one-bedroom apartment is too small for the three of us, therefore we shall spend every waking moment looking for a new place. It is getting really hard working full time, scrambling to find a place suitable for our little prince before he comes and preparing to have a baby in our lives all at the same time. I am beginning to swell up really bad and it seems as though this belly is getting heavier and heavier by the minute! Baby is due September 24 so we do not have much time to find a new place and get settled before our baby is here. The stress is beginning to pile up.

July 9, 2013

Today makes 29 weeks into my pregnancy and the apps say baby is about the size of a butternut squash and also about 15.7 inches long. These apps are so fun to read, it gives me an idea of what baby is doing and how he is growing. Although I should be looking for a place to stay, I am in full baby mode and I cannot stop thinking about how I am going to be a mom soon. Baby shower is August 10 and we are going for a taste testing soon to try out the food. Yummy! I cannot wait. This is my favorite part of planning a party. This time my wife is doing all of the work as I sit back and make the easy decisions.

In July, I was 29 weeks pregnant, my son was growing hair on his head, and as per my pregnancy applications he was about the size of a butternut squash. I wonder if he we have a lot of hair. I don't get heartburn at all. I wonder, too, if that is just another pregnancy myth. I am so large now that I can no longer see my toes.

July 13, 2013

You would think that because it is a Saturday that I get to rest. You would be wrong. My wife thinks she found a nice place and wants to go take a look. With our baby coming in just over two months we have to move quickly. So off we go to check out this place and well, I just cannot stop stressing about how quickly everything is happening. We will begin packing up this weekend if all goes well with this new place. In other news, I am constantly drinking water, which means frequent trips to the restroom. If my other half is home that means I have to be a swift bathroom warrior since there is only one bathroom. Why does she always have to go when I do? Always at the same time, really? No, you wait! I am the one with the big round belly! I *should have bathroom privileges! This new location better have two bathrooms.*

Denise said she might have found the perfect place for us to move into. We both wanted to go take a look and see if it was the one. I hope out loud that the new place has two bathrooms, because we are constantly vying for the bathroom at the same time! *What's her excuse?* I wonder, also out loud.

July 14, 2013

Great news! This new place is the perfect fit. Almost perfect for our growing family! I say almost because we really did not want to move into a condo, as you know how condominium associations can be. I feel like this is the only option. Time is limited as we race to move into our new place before our baby is finally here! Not to mention the baby shower is in just a few weeks and we need a place to put all of the new baby things. Speaking of the baby, we have finally decided on his name! I am so excited; all I seem to do is write his name over and over on any blank piece of paper I can find. Well don't think too hard! You will find out his name when he arrives! I like keeping you on your toes.

The place turned out to be perfect. It is a two-bedroom and, yes, you've guessed it, a two-bathroom condominium. It has a nice balcony and it is located in a very quiet and family friendly complex.

As we completed our packing and my wife started moving boxes downstairs into the moving van, I found a small sticky pad and a pen. In a daydream, I wrote my son's name over and over until there was no space left. This is not the first, nor the last time, time I would do this. I find it to be relaxing.

Slowly, our apartment starts to look the way it did when we first moved in and nothing is in its place anymore. The plan was to move in to our new place on August 1, but the old owners were nice enough to give us access early so we could start moving our things before then. Soon, the only things left in our apartment were the air mattress and bare necessities. Unable to help her in my state, my wife has spent her nights moving all of these heavy boxes into the new place, by herself. I cannot sleep without her by my side.

At thirty weeks into my pregnancy, the baby's lungs and digestive tract are almost fully developed. I only had about ten weeks left to go! I was really excited for the upcoming classes at the hospital – one on CPR and another on breastfeeding and parenting 101.

July 25, 2013
Talk about being exhausted! I am still working full time with no time to relax. Our apartment is completely empty besides the

air mattress and a couple of boxes on the living room floor. My wife has been going back and forth to the new place during the evening to move everything on her own. I feel horrible because I cannot help her with the heavy things and I cannot sleep without here by my side. Who knew that moving and working full time while in your third trimester would be so stressful? Today actually makes 31 weeks into my pregnancy and I only have about 9 weeks left to go. Aside from all of the stress, I cannot wait to meet my little prince.

August 1, 2013

Today I am 32 weeks pregnant and we have pretty much everything done with the move. Yay! We are officially in our new home and there is just one thing left to do, unpack. Now this I can definitely help with. However, I am not so sure I am up for the challenge. Today is my day off from work but I cannot even sit for five minutes. We have the furniture being delivered and the carpets will be cleaned this weekend. Not to mention, the nursery has to be completed! You can imagine how stressful this is for a woman who is carrying a baby in her belly, which just happens to be the size of a basketball! At least I get to sleep in my own bed again. I am tired of waking up to leg cramps in the middle of the night. They are the worst!

August 7, 2013

Going into my 33rd week of pregnancy, I am starting to notice a lot of changes. I read on my apps that it can be due to stress so I am trying my best to take it easy but it doesn't seem to be going so well. I am also swelling up really bad. It even hurts to walk and if I poke my skin, you can see the imprint of my finger. I see my doctor on Friday and I have a ton of questions. I called the office and they advised me to take it slow. How can I? That is not possible. I am still working full time and the nursery is not quite complete. I wonder who is going to put this crib together?

At 32 weeks, my belly is the size of a basketball, probably bigger, and it just would not stop itching! I was constantly rubbing coconut oil on my belly but it didn't seem to work. Although I found that warm water does the trick, I couldn't exactly walk around with warm water on my belly all day. At 33 weeks, it took far too long to walk up the three flights of stairs to my new home. I felt constantly out of breath, with headaches as well. This could be due to all of the stress. The applications on my phone said stress often causes headaches.

At my next appointment, the doctor told Denise and I that my blood pressure was too high and the swelling was a concern. I may have developed preeclampsia but to be sure he was sending me for an emergency appointment with a specialist. After this check-up I had to go straight to the specialist's office where they confirmed that I did indeed have preeclampsia. I needed a two dose shot to speed up the development of my baby's lungs because I found that I may be forced into an emergency cesarean section as well as a premature labor. I remember the shock that I felt as the specialist began to explain what preeclampsia is and if it was not treated in the correct manner it could become a more permanent problem.

I was scared. I didn't know what to expect and what would come next. She told me she could give me the first shot right then and there but I had to go to the hospital for the second shot the next day, since it was Friday and her office would be closed on Saturday. I cried. I was so frustrated and was becoming angry. The entire pregnancy was too good to be true. I knew it. I had only gained about nine pounds the first two trimesters and then in the last few weeks gained well over 20 pounds. I had placed too much stress on myself these past few weeks and I did way more than what I should have. I pushed myself too much and now I had caused strain on my pregnancy. Clearly, I was also beating myself up for the situation I had landed myself in. Looking at my wife, I can see that she was just as nervous and I was. We briefly discussed it and agreed it was the best thing for me to do. I signed the documents and pulled down my pants as instructed just enough for her to give me the corticosteroid shot to speed up the growth of the lungs. I had no idea what was about to happen next.

Although that shot only took a few seconds of my time, time seemed to stand still. I was frozen and honestly cannot tell you how long I stared at that wall. Pure fear ran through my entire body. I felt bare, exposed, defenseless and most of all I felt entirely helpless. Nothing was in my control. Was my baby even okay? They said the shot would do no harm at all and would help the baby develop lungs at a rapid pace in case I do had to be induced. Induced. For labor. I was not ready for this. I still had six weeks left to go in this pregnancy. I didn't realize that I had lost myself in that moment. I could not hear or see anything. My body was trembling and my eyes filled with tears.

Then finally I heard the doctor calling my name, "Christina, are you okay?" I could not find the words to say what I felt.

I simply responded, " Yes, thank you doctor. Where should I go for the second shot?" I looked at my wife who had a worried look in her eyes. The realization hit at this very moment that our fairytale pregnancy had been interrupted by reality. I only know the pain I felt in that very moment and could not find it in myself to observe the energy I had projected onto my wife. I knew we had to be strong but how can we be?

As per the doctor's orders, I was placed on leave from work and put on bed rest. Is this even a thing at this point in time? *But I still have to unpack!* My mind screamed. *I have to put the crib together, and tomorrow is supposed to be my baby shower!*

Listening to the stories of other mothers I have met during this journey, I used to think to myself, *Oh wow, I wonder if she is exaggerating her experience or if it was really this bad?* Now I knew the answer. The next day, as I waited for the nurse to call my name, I realized that my leg had been shaking uncontrollably. When it was finally my turn, I took the shot like a champ. As I prepared to leave and get ready for my baby shower, the nurse stopped me, explaining that I couldn't leave yet.

Chills ran through my body as she told me that my blood

pressure was very high and I may need an emergency C-section. I didn't even realize the tears streaming down my face as she shoved papers in front of me. Her mouth moved but no sound seemed to come out. Everything piled on top of me one by one and I felt suffocated. I was not only very upset but I was hurt and confused. I was angry.

"Just give me a minute to think!" I blurted out. I felt horrible for yelling at her and as she walked away, I just looked at my wife so helpless. For the first time ever in my life, I simply did not have the answers. No smart remarks, no arrogant come backs, no planning... I had nothing. Having a C-section was never an option for me. I wanted to have a natural birth. If I had a C-section, I wouldn't be able to hold my son when he is born. How would my body react to this procedure?

My mind wouldn't settle. *I feel fine, why are they telling me this? These are the people who are going to deliver my child and this is what they tell me? How can I trust them? Do I even have any options?* I was angry so very angry and each minute I had to wait for the nurse to return became more and more aggravating for me. When she finally did come back the first thing she asked is if I had signed the papers. No! I did not sign these damned papers. I needed to know what my options were! At this point my mind was racing and I was unable to think straight. I was waiting for my wife to speak up and say something, anything but she never did. She was silent and it scared me even more. Typically, I am vocal but she is the more extroverted one. It wasn't until this very moment that I realized every ounce of pain, frustration and fear I was expressing verbally and emotionally, she was soaking in and hiding it inside. It was as though our roles had switched and I knew I had to take control. I asked the nurse two questions. "Is my son okay?" and "If I decide against this emergency C-section am I putting his life in danger?"

The nurse then explained that my blood pressure had gone back down to normal but if it came back up again and stayed high, I would not have a choice. I know some of you reading this will probably think I am insane and irresponsible and others may frown upon it, but as mothers we really do not know what we are doing the first time around. We make decisions that are based on our gut feelings and we go by instinct. There is something built inside of us that we spend all of our lives silently and internally preparing for and do not realize what that something is until we have a child. With that being said, my blood pressure had been normal for some time now as the nurse had me hooked up to a monitor and was able to keep an eye on my blood pressure. I was informed that the baby is still healthy and safe, I felt completely fine besides this situation with preeclampsia that had arisen so I used my judgment as a woman and a mother to sign myself of out hospital.

After finally getting released, we headed straight for the hotel to attend my baby shower. The car was completely quiet besides my crying. Denise just grabbed my hand and at that moment it was exactly what I needed. No words were necessary. I just needed to know that we were in this together. I no longer felt alone. I knew that at that moment that I had her support and we would get through this.

Baby Shower Time!

When we arrived at the hotel, the hostess informed me that my dress and makeup were in a nearby room and the guests had arrived and are here waiting for me. I hadn't realized how late we were. She pointed to the room where my dress and other things were. I looked down at myself. I was wearing a red and white striped shirt, yoga pants, and a hospital band on my wrist. I knew my friends and family had been waiting for some time, and would be wondering why we were so late. I thought to myself, *I am about to celebrate the coming of my son with the people I hold closest to my heart. I am going through something serious and I am not going to hide this moment. I always keep everything so private.* I looked over at my wife, nodded my head, and walked right into the event room, just as I was.

My eyes swollen from all of the crying that day, and the tears continued to roll down my cheek. I tried to speak but the words just would not come out. Denise jumped in to explain to our guests what was going on and why we were late. There was a very brief silence and then, just like that all of those people that I love so much began clapping and shouting they love me. I got tons of hugs and whispers of how strong I am. For the first time ever, for those first few minutes,

I let all of those people in. I let them into my most private moments and there was nothing but pure love and support. I exhaled a large sigh of relief.

After our meal, I watched as my guests played the games. Everyone participated and I laughed as they all enjoyed themselves. I took plenty of pictures and videos of them making fools of themselves but we enjoyed every second of it. People were blindfolded and trying to feed each other baby food. Others were wrapping each other in toilet paper trying to create the best adult diaper. In those few moments, I felt pure joy. At each event I attend I always do one thing: I secretly take a step back from everybody and everything and I just observe. I soak in all of the happiness and positivity that fills the place. For that time, I am present. I am in that moment and I keep those memories locked in a special part of my mind. Those pure moments are the ones that fill my heart. These are the special moments that keep me going when I have no fuel left.

We ate cake and laughed together. As the hostess began handing out the favors for the baby shower, our guests began taking pictures with me. I remember trying to hide the hospital band in each picture. I almost made it to the end of the shower. I am not sure if standing in one spot to take pictures with so many people was becoming overwhelming but I know I started to feel dizzy. I needed to sit down and relax. I had been through so much that day and I needed to take a break. Then I realized the feeling of dizziness did not go away and it was time to get back to the hospital. We were supposed to stay at the hotel along with some guests who traveled to be there for our special moment, but instead, we ended up leaving the shower a little early. My wife announced to our guests that I was not feeling well and we had to make our way back to the hospital.

When we got to the hospital the nurse immediately took me in and hooked me up to the machine. She called a doctor in to explain to me that I needed a C-section since my blood pressure had gone up again. After being in the room for a couple of hours I watched as my blood pressure went up and down. I was only 34 weeks and two days pregnant. It was too early to give birth! I still had almost six weeks left to go. The doctor came in again with the nurse to ask if I would sign the papers for the C-section now. Something in my gut kept telling me to hold on.

"Is the baby okay?" I asked the doctor. "Are there any risks in me waiting this out?" The doctor explained that the baby was not showing any signs of distress and if I could keep my blood pressure at a normal rate then it would be okay if I waited. Each day counted. I guess after some time, they realized that I was not giving up on my body just yet. The nurse made a deal with me so to speak. She said since my blood pressure was normal for some time now, if I can maintain a normal pressure then they would release me. So we waited. I was nervous and scared but after about two hours my blood pressure did not change significantly enough to be a cause for concern. I felt fine and I knew that if I went home, I would be happy with that decision. I was not giving up on having a natural labor. My baby was not in jeopardy in any type of way, so I wanted to leave. After three hours, I called the nurse back in.

To my surprise she did not stick to her end of the deal and she returned with the papers for the C-section yet again and told me I had to sign them. I felt at this point it was a game they were playing. I know hospitals make more money off of doing a cesarean section and they often push patients to get opt into this procedure for this reason alone. They didn't give me any reasons as to why I should sign these papers. They just kept telling me the baby is safe and healthy. My blood pressure had been normal for hours. So why would I sign them? I felt fine and I really wanted to get out of those clothes and out of that hospital. So I did what I wanted to and asked for release papers yet again.

We made our way back to the hotel and I realized that I had not finished eating my meal earlier that day. I was starving! We went to the hotel and checked into our room then headed out with my cousin to get some food. It was nearly the middle of the night but we didn't care. When we returned to my hotel room, I noticed all of the gifts for the first time. I felt like a child on Christmas morning. It was so much fun going through all of the presents. As I opened each one, I secretly imagined where in the nursery it would go.

What Happens Next

The next morning as we checked out of the hotel, our best friends from Florida came back to our condo with us and helped put the crib together. The crib, still in pieces and boxes, had been haunting me, and our friends' offer to build it was a huge relief. The crib was up in a couple of hours and we started putting other things together to complete the nursery. I even found this cool wall decal that had the baby's name and a beautiful saying. We decided to place that just above the crib. I couldn't have been more thankful for this weekend and our friends and family than I was at that moment. For the first time in months I felt as though everything was finally coming together. I was able to relax for the first time in a while.

Later that night I woke up in the middle of night with trouble breathing. All I was doing was lying in the bed, but I was short of breath. I got out of bed and walked around the condo with a glass of water, but nothing I did took the feeling away. I got in the shower thinking maybe the water would calm me down. It could just be anxiety from all of the events that had occurred over the past few days. When I got out of the shower, I realized that I still could not breathe properly so I knew it was time. I woke my wife up and explained what was going on. She jumped out of bed and ran around frantically trying to get things ready for us to go. She even called the police department to give them our plates and let them know we would be passing through the lights on our way to the emergency room. It was quite the dramatic experience. I was nervous and didn't understand what was going on.

In the hospital I learned that this was all because of the preeclampsia. With preeclampsia you retain water my body was swelling up. Preeclampsia is also sometimes referred to as toxemia. Some common symptoms are fatigue, headaches, nausea, and you guessed, it shortness of breath. I had every single one of those symptoms; I had just been too busy to realize it. Toxemia can also slow the blood flow to the placenta, which I later found out, could result in the baby being born underweight. The reason for this is because it interferes with the oxygen and even the food your baby gets. Being in the hospital this time was different. I knew in my heart I had to listen to what the doctors were telling me. I finally gave in and allowed them to hook me up to the machine and proceed with doing whatever tests they needed to perform to make sure my son and I would both be okay.

I asked my wife to call my mother to let her know I was in the hospital and this time I was staying. Nurses were coming and going all day. I also spoke to a couple of different doctors. It seemed as though everyone was pushing a cesarean section on me but I refused to have the procedure done if my son's life was not at risk. I remember one doctor came into the room; she was a young woman. She checked my vitals and asked me, "Do you want to have a natural birth?" I confirmed that I indeed wanted to push this little munchkin out on my own and she promised me she would do everything she could to help me accomplish that.

Sometime in the early evening, the doctor explained that they needed to induce me. They returned a few hours later to induce me with a Foley Balloon, and after that the nurses would come and go for the next few hours to check on how I was progressing. I was starting to feel contractions coming but they were far apart. One of the doctors said my labor was not progressing quickly enough and they decided to place another balloon inside of my vagina. The second one hurt as much as the first one did and I really wanted to scream at them for doing it! The pain turned into anger and I was growing impatient by the minute. I knew I had to calm down so I let my thoughts of holding my precious bundle of joy keep me sane. During all of this chaos I felt as though I was losing my mind but every time I thought of seeing his face for the first time, it brought me back to a calm state of mind.

I drifted in and out of sleep until the contractions really started coming on strong. I looked over and my wife was literally sleeping on the windowsill. My mom was fast asleep on the chair next to me. I do not remember the exact time but I know those contractions were hitting me back to back and it was hard to catch my breath. I yelled, "I have to push! I have to push!" My wife jumped up and told me to go back to bed while my mom got up and started walking towards the door. Before she could get out the room the nurse came in and then ran back out to get the doctor. I felt my body and I knew this was it!

I didn't know how it happened but when you are in labor and ready to push, a switch inside of you immediately turns on and you realize it is happening. You automatically know what to do. I cannot explain it but the doctor checked me and said I was ten plus one and then quickly proceeded with breaking my water. As she did so, the fluid came shooting out of me and got all over the bed and floor. I felt a warm sensation down below and then another contraction came on.

The doctor told me that on the count of three she wanted me to push. She counted to three; I took a deep breath, put my chin to my chest and pushed. I didn't really know how to push but once I did for the first time, I felt it. I felt the baby moving through my birth canal and knew that I needed to use my belly to push. The second contraction was coming and the doctor told me to get ready to push again. So again I took a deep breath, brought my chin to my chest and I pushed! This time I felt my son moving closer and I heard the nurses saying they see the head coming. I felt a rush of energy and excitement, fear and happiness all at the same time.

It wasn't until that moment I realized that there were nurses from the NICU there. The room was literally filled with people. I really didn't have time to think the next one through. Denise was at my side and all I was thinking was that I wanted this to be over. I was scared and nervous. The emotions I was experiencing were at an all-time high. I felt another contraction coming and although the doctor yelled not to push, I did it anyway. I couldn't hold it back even though I tried. Then, there he was. My precious little angel made his way into the world and all of the chaos immediately ceased. He was out.

My son was just born! Isaiah is here! I sat back and took a few deep breaths, tears flowing down my face as my wife cut the umbilical cord. I was waiting to hear his cries to let me know he was okay. My heart skipped a beat and chills just ran through my body.

Then it hit me... *He isn't crying. Why isn't he crying?* I asked if he was okay but the nurses were too busy cleaning him and doing whatever they were doing. All I knew at that moment was that the noise had stopped and there was silence. All I heard were the NICU nurses whispering as they cleaned him up. My wife had already cut the umbilical cord and the doctor was instructing me to push the placenta out. Too many things were happening at once and then time froze for just a second. My baby shouted out so loudly that he was here. He cried and kept on crying until they wrapped him up in a blanket. He was so precious. I wanted to hold him so badly but the nurses were all over him.

It was then that I had realized I only made it 34 weeks and six days before giving birth to my munchkin. It was 3:20am on Wednesday August 14, and I had just given birth to a beautiful baby boy. The nurse brought him over to me and said, "Look at your baby boy." Then she turned him toward me so I can look at him. I knew they had to take him to the NICU for testing, but not without me holding him first. I took him right from her hands and held him close for as long as they allowed me to, which wasn't long at all. I gave him lots of kisses and told him I loved him so much but he was already sleeping. I thought to myself, so *this is what heaven feels like*. I did not want to let him go but I knew I had to. What happened next was another story.

The Aftermath

The doctors wouldn't let me get up from the bed and they didn't bring my son back to me either. My wife and mom took turns going back to the NICU to see the baby but I wasn't able to see him. They kept pumping magnesium into my IV and I think I may have gotten a reaction from it because I broke out in little tiny bumps everywhere. Every time a doctor or nurse left the room, a new one came in to administer something different into the IV. I felt like a lab rat. I swore they were out to punish me for signing myself out of the hospital and they would not allow me to get up from the bed and see my baby. They would not even allow me to sit up or have any water.

A full day went by and I still had not seen him. I begged for my mom and wife to stay with me. They were not allowed to leave me alone. Finally, on Friday, a doctor came in and was discussing my chart with a couple of the nurses and residents that had been in and out of the room all day and I blurted out, "Can I just get some water and sit up!" It wasn't even a question. It was a very firm statement letting the doctor know that I was not happy with what was going on. It was at that moment he told them to remove the catheter and get me some water and ice chips.

I knew that my son doing well because my wife had been updating me but inside I was jealous and upset. I was going through so many emotions. I just wanted to be able to see and hold my baby. I felt confused and sad at the same time. I had given birth on Wednesday morning at 3:20am. It was nearly midnight on Friday and I was finally able to get up from the bed. After being bed ridden for nearly three days it was a bit tough for me to walk across the hospital to the NICU to see my precious baby but nothing was stopping me. I took my time and it took all of the strength I had but I made it. Nothing else mattered at that moment. I was finally able to see my baby. He was in an incubator because he had jaundice due to being premature. He was long but very skinny. He weighed 3 lbs and 13.5 oz. He was 21 inches long!

As I stood there holding his tiny little hand, I received updates on what was going on the past couple of days without me. Supposedly they tried putting a feeding tube up his nose but he was not having it and yanked it right out. He couldn't have my breast milk because of the magnesium so they ended up giving him formula which I was not happy about at all but I didn't have a choice so I quickly let that one go. He also kept pulling at his eye mask during phototherapy. He was quite the rebel to only be three days old.

I could not stop staring at him. He was perfect and he was here. The nurses in the NICU were so very friendly and informative. They even let me hold him through their shift change. I spent quite some time with him and took plenty of pictures and videos. I was falling in love so quickly. He even smiled at me. He made me regain my strength and I knew at that moment that I would do anything for him. Eventually I had to head back to my room to get cleaned up and also to pump some milk for him. I promised him that I would take care of myself and come right back.

Later, the doctor came in the room to evaluate me and let me know I would be going home the next day. I was really happy to get that news however that happiness quickly dissipated once I learned Joseph would not be coming with me. This brought feelings that I could not understand. Part of me was upset and very hurt and on the other hand I blamed myself. Surely there had to be something wrong with me that my child was born early and was not able to come home with his mother. I did not realize at this point I was changing. My mind was changing. I did not look at myself the same. I was growing an anger towards myself that later on would become something more serious.

There were a couple of visitors that day and although I was very thankful they took the time to come by and see how Joseph and I were doing, I really just wanted to be left alone. I couldn't imagine going home without my son. The past week had been a very difficult one, and I didn't know how I was going to gather the strength to leave this hospital without my newborn. I literally spent every second that I could with Isaiah the next day as I prepared myself to leave without him. But he would have to stay in the NICU until he hit the four-pound mark. If he were anything like me, he would not be here much longer.

Leaving the Hospital Without Him...

The day you leave the hospital as a first-time mother is supposed to be a joyous one, but as I walked to the car, the warm air on my face, I fought back tears. I heard Denise talking to me in the background but I couldn't really make out what she was saying. My mind drifted and I immediately regretted leaving without my baby boy. My stomach turned into knots and my nerves were getting the best of me. I pulled out my phone and started looking at the pictures I had taken the past couple of days. The ride home was very quiet or at least I thought it was. I could not hear anything and my vision seemed to have been a blur. My heart was breaking and there wasn't anything I could do about it. I started to feel like this was entirely my fault. What kind of mother was I, at home without my baby?

When I reached home I realized my breasts were feeling very heavy and getting a bit hard. I pumped and to my surprise I had produced milk. Although I was feeling very sad about not having my son home with me, I knew this was something I had to stay on top of for him. So I was determined to pump every three hours around the clock. I wasn't getting a lot of milk either and with the size of my breasts being so big, I thought my milk supply would not be an issue at all. I did not understand why I was coming up short, but I did not give up. Watching as my milk filled the bottles, I felt that not all hope was lost and this would all be worth it.

I went to visit Isaiah in the hospital every single day and spent as much time with him as they allowed me to. I held him and spoke to him. I changed his diaper and was able to help bathe him. I was a little nervous changing his diaper for the first time but it seemed to come naturally to me. Helping my mother with all of the dirty diapers growing up paid off. I watched as he grew little by little and his skin started to gain its natural color. When I went home at night, the NICU would send me emails with his bilirubin levels and to let me know when he used the bathroom, ate, and did anything new. I really only went home to shower and change. I ate on the way to the hospital and did not spend any time doing anything else. I pumped when I was at home and brought the milk with me to the hospital. Isaiah loved his breast milk and the nurses assured me it was helping him to grow. They were so supportive but it really didn't change the fact that I had to leave the hospital without him over and over again for the next 14 days. Each time was just as bad as the first time. I did appreciate the support of the nurses and how they kept me up to date with his every move. Although I was thankful, it was also a reminder every time they reached out that he was there and I was home. I did not sleep much at all during this time. I knew I was going through something but I didn't have any time to figure it out.

One afternoon, I decided to take a quick shower before Denise came back and we would head over to the hospital again. In the shower I started crying, I let out a loud scream and the crying increased. I knew I had to pull myself together. I cried for a few more minutes before I turned the water off and got dressed. The next two weeks were all about my son and getting him out of the hospital. Even though I felt as if I were letting myself down, I had to keep pushing forward. I didn't have time to try to piece together what was going on with me. I just wanted to bring him home.

The nurses made a big announcement: he had passed the four-pound mark and would be ready to come home soon! He had to complete some more testing and evaluations but as long as he passed the car seat test, he would be released. During the car seat test, the nurses place the baby in a car seat strap him in securely, then monitor his oxygen levels and heart rate for about 90 minutes. If all is well at the end of the test then your baby will be allowed to use the car seat and head home. When I received the news, I remember being so happy that I cried in the hospital. The tears were a little bit of everything. They were sadness because I still had to wait a couple more days, happiness that I would not have to visit the hospital again, and excitement to have my baby in my arms and in the comfort of my own home, his home.

Although he had been in the NICU all of this time I was thankful that he was in good hands. I trusted the nurses to care for him. He was in good health but he just had to sort out a couple of things before he came home to me and that was okay. During his stay in the hospital the rest of the umbilical cord had fallen off. The nurse was saving it for me and when I arrived she asked me if I wanted to keep it or if I wanted her to toss it. I looked at it and it was really just a piece of dried up stuff that looked a little weird so I told her she can toss it. I watched her as she tossed it in the trash and I felt a knot in my stomach when she did it. I had realized that was the last piece that physically held him and me together and it was now in the trash. I quashed the desire to dive head first into the trash to get it.

Finally Home

On August 28, my little angel was allowed to come home as long as he passed the car seat test. My wife and I dressed him in his going home outfit and waited for the nurses to bring him to another section of the neonatal intensive care unit. I was so excited that I could not stop smiling. I really just wanted to get this over with and flee the hospital with our baby in tow. During this process, I had to fill out a ton of paperwork and speak to the nurses about our son leaving the hospital.

The time seemed to have been dragging for some reason so that is when I sat back and took a good look around me. I had been in this NICU with my son for what seemed to be an eternity and I rarely associated with any of the other mothers there. Some babies only weighed one pound at birth while others had been in the neonatal intensive care unit for months on end. As I waited for the nurse to finish the car seat test, I took the time to reflect on my short journey. I had watched parents cry because they were not able to hold their babies, mothers become frustrated that their babies were there for a very long time, losing hope of their babies making it home. I had witnessed couples fighting because they did not know how to come together and handle their journey. This moment helped me to understand just how precious my son was and how proud I was of him for fighting so hard to gain weight and get healthy. He did it all without having my cuddles throughout the night or his moms to sing him a lullaby.

But now I was just thankful. I was thankful our journey in the NICU was a short one. He was just two weeks old. I was thankful that he was now fully healthy and he was finally coming home. I prayed for the other parents still in the NICU and their babies. I silently wished them good health in short time and hoped they would soon be walking out the hospital with their babies in hand just like I was. I hoped that every mother would soon be able to feel this joy because every mother in the world deserves to be able to take her baby home.

Isaiah passed the car seat test and was able to leave the hospital right after. Words cannot express how I felt as I signed him out of the hospital. I was filled with joy and excitement. At the same time, I was nervous and worried if I would be good enough for him. I was anxious to get him home. I did not want think about the hospital at all. As we put him in the car seat, I decided to sit in the back with him as my wife drove us home. Staring at him sleeping the entire way home, I was falling in love with him all over again. I also felt bad as I noticed he scratched his forehead. I told myself it should go away in a few days and really didn't think about it again. You would think we were brand new drivers because she was driving about 15 miles per hour. It was hilarious. We eventually made it home and brought him upstairs to his new home. It was at this moment our new place felt complete. The whole reason we moved into the condo was for him. I felt relieved knowing everything was already unpacked and his nursery was already set up. I did not have to do anything but try to catch up on some much-needed sleep and pump milk for my little prince.

Once upstairs we made him comfortable and got him out of the clothes he left the hospital in. I held him for a long time and was so thankful that he finally made it home. The last couple of weeks had been so rough but right now none of that mattered. All that mattered was that he was home and healthy.

We put him in his crib to sleep and saw how tiny he looked in that big crib. We looked at each other and it must have looked like a scene from a movie as I picked him up and my wife assembled the playpen. It had a bassinet attached to the top and he fit perfectly in it. We placed it right next to our bed and knew that he was not only safe but also easily accessible to us if he needed to be changed or fed throughout the night. Was this a first-time mommy mistake? I am not sure but it was definitely our first mommy moment. We quickly learned that there would be many more of these to come.

Having him home was amazing! We shared so many laughs and looked up so many things on the internet. The classes we had taken at the hospital could not prepare us enough for having our little prince home. He was perfect and I wanted to capture every single moment. They say you are supposed to sleep when the baby sleeps but I would love to know how many mothers actually do this. Perhaps a second time mom would be a pro at this but I was still a rookie and laughed at the thought of sleeping as he was sleeping. How could I? He looked so perfect I could not keep my eyes off of him. There were a few times I can remember dozing off but then he would make a sound and I immediately woke up. Even if I was cleaning or cooking or doing anything else but staring at his handsome little face, once he made a sound I was rushing right to the bedroom. This is the part that mothers do not talk about. Everyone says how fun it is and how beautiful the experience is. Nobody ever talks about the embarrassing or scary moments. It is these times moms need to be more open in talking about because we first time mothers need to be prepared for this stuff!

    With our son finally home we decided to allow close family and friends to come visit after he got his shots. Until then he was all ours. Although he was home and easily adjusting, I realized I still was not getting any sleep. Nights would pass and I would be up all night. I continued to pump as I got him acclimated to breast-feeding which was a challenge in itself. He did not latch on at first and it took a lot of practice and patience. When he finally did latch, he would end up crying and I believe it could have been because I was not producing enough milk. I tried pretty much everything and although I was still pumping around the clock it did not seem like enough. This had become such a stressful time. I felt as though I was failing. I was very hard on myself. I also noticed the scratch on his forehead was getting larger and I did not understand it. Since I could not sleep at night I spent this time researching what this red mark could be. You know how they say never look up your symptoms when you are sick? I never listen and always have to learn things the hard way. So many different things were coming up during my search, not to mention the pictures that scared me half to death. I could not wait for his first pediatric appointment.

Laser What?

During his first appointment with the pediatrician we learned it could be what they call a hemangioma. His pediatrician says it is common in children and more commonly recognized by the name strawberry mark. She recommended we wait for him to hit his one-year mark and then see a specialist if it did not stop growing. At first, we took her advice thinking it would get better or at least stay the same size. I realized the more time that had passed, the more this hemangioma began protruding and growing larger. I was scared because it was in the middle of his forehead right between his eyes. I did not know how big it was going to get but I will tell you one thing: it did not stop growing and I was not waiting any longer. I called the pediatrician and asked her for a few recommendations to see a specialist. I needed to get a consultation as quickly as possible. I spoke with many doctors over the phone who recommended we wait so I did not stop calling until we found a specialist in New York City who was willing to see Joseph. We set up the consultation and starting making calls to the insurance company.

During the consultation the specialist confirmed that it is indeed a hemangioma. He informed us that he normally recommends waiting to see if it will go away on its own but because it was growing rapidly he wanted to start treatment right away. Our little man was just shy of two months old when we made the decision to proceed with the Pulsed Dye Laser Treatments. He would have to come every two weeks and the treatments were very brief. Insurance tried to say it was a cosmetic procedure so that was yet another hurdle we had to jump. While we waited for the first treatment, we saw children there much older than our son. Some children had this hemangioma all over one side of their body or all over their face, another child had it on the whole left side of his body and leg.

The parents were all curious about our baby and how we were able to start treatments so young. In speaking with these parents we learned one thing: their children's hemangiomas started off significantly small and increased in size as they took the advice of their pediatricians. Wait for the first year and see if it goes away on its own. I remember another first-time mother we met there told us her daughters strawberry mark started off just a little bigger than our baby's and she waited. Now it was the size of her earlobe and continues to grow. With these treatments the strawberry mark is supposed to stop growing and become flat again. We hoped it would fade away completely.

We had to lay Joseph down on the bed and place goggles on him and ourselves. The doctor lowered the machine as the nurse turned off the light and the process began. They only gave him three rounds, which are about two seconds each. The specialist gave us a special cream to put on the mark and it would be the same thing each time. At first the mark kept growing but the doctor was confident and assured us the process is working. Each time we went Joseph cried for a few seconds and then was back to his normal and happy self as soon as it was over. The skin became bruised around the hemangioma due to the laser but it went away after a couple of days. It did not seem to hurt him at all, which was a relief. These laser treatments went on every other week for about eight months. After his last treatment, you could barely see the mark, but he still did have a small bump on his forehead. The specialist said it should not be a cause for concern, as he will grow into it. By his first birthday the mark was completely gone and the bump was getting smaller without any further treatments. We were completely happy with the results.

How is Mommy?

When Joseph was born, I blamed myself for him being born early. I blamed myself for everything. What hit me the hardest was not being able to see him those first few days and then having to leave the hospital without him. When I left the hospital something inside of me changed. I felt that I had failed my child as a mother and I did not feel adequate enough. Some nights I even felt that I had abandoned him in the hospital. I didn't take care of myself because I was so caught up in the negativity. When he finally did come home, I was completely overprotective. I didn't want him to go anywhere without me or be out of sight. If he wasn't near me, even for a few minutes I would get anxiety and had to find my way to him.

I fought with Denise about pretty much everything. I did not want to see anyone, I did not sleep, and I often felt down and did not feel happy to be a mother. I secretly cried, a lot. I was not opening up about how I felt or what I was going through. This whole time I kept this all inside. Although, there were quite a few times where I allowed these feelings to cloud my judgment and it caused a heavy burden on my marriage. I did not realize at the time that I was going through postpartum depression. During my first postpartum check up with my primary care physician, she asked questions about how I was feeling and as I was explaining to her what I had been going through, she told me these were all signs of postpartum depression and wanted me to seek professional help.

I remember being confused about the outcome of the appointment with my primary care physician. Postpartum depression? There have been stories on the news, movies and television shows about how mothers who develop postpartum depression hurt themselves or their babies. To be honest, I was scared. Not to mention seeking professional health was something that I was against. Due to my lack of knowledge in how important mental health is, I was hesitant in seeing someone I didn't know and tell them my deepest worries and feelings. Something inside of me told me that if I did not handle this issue head on, it could lead to something worse. I did not want to ruin my experience as a mother nor did I want to shortchange my newborn child because I was not taking care of myself. I knew this was something I had to do. I was not okay. So I set up an appointment to speak with a therapist.

The first appointment was awkward. I am a naturally quiet

person especially if I am just meeting you for the first time. How in the world am I supposed to open my heart to someone I do not know? It was quite intimidating. I left the office with not much progress and I had to set up another appointment. I didn't really speak about anything important or how I felt. I simply updated the therapist on what was going on toward the end of the pregnancy and through labor. I was discouraged and almost felt stupid for even signing up to speak with a specialist. It was even a little embarrassing but I had to give her a chance. She did ask how it made me feel but my response was that I did not know how I felt. It was an honest answer. I was trying to ignore the pain and frustration. I did not realize the substantial impact these feelings held on my life. She said she wanted to talk about it more during the next week's session. I started seeing the therapist once a week. During the second appointment I opened up a little more and by the third session I found it even easier to speak to her. Little by little, as time went on, I was talking about it all. She did confirm my primary care physician's suspicions about me going through postpartum depression and brought comfort in teaching me that it was a normal process some mothers go through. She told me I was also going through separation anxiety. The two things are both different and very real. She assured me this feeling would not last forever and she would help me get through this. I was happy to know someone understood how I felt and was there to support me through the process. Soon I found myself looking forward to these weekly sessions. There was no judgment on her end and she seemed to take her time to educate me on what I was going through. It helped me to understand why I was feeling the way I was and how to process it as opposed to internalizing it.

As time went on, I began to feel more confident and comfortable in knowing that taking care of myself was indeed helping me. I was beginning to see the light through this dark time I had been going through. Little by little I was finding myself again. I was able to communicate my feelings in an effective way instead of using anger. I even found myself laughing and smiling again. I realized how much these weekly sessions were helping and how I was changing. This time I was changing for the better. It took me some time to get to a better place and a full understanding of what I was going through but with patience and an open mind I did get there. It wasn't until then that I realized just how strong I was. Not only as a woman but also as a mother. This was a pivotal moment in my growth process. It took nearly two years to get passed my emotional insecurities and mental setbacks. The best part is that I got through it. I was so proud of myself. Not to mention I felt better! I mean I still worried about my son but I think as a mother this is natural. I am not sure that will ever go away.

I cannot stress enough how important it is to get help. Therapy is just as important as getting your blood work done to make sure you are physically healthy during your annual check-ups. I do not think there is enough support around mental health. I was born in the 80's, raised in New York City in the 90's and early 2000's and nobody that I grew up with ever went to see a therapist. Nobody ever spoke about his or her issues, and not many people sought out help, not even from other family members. I was taught to grow a strong backbone and use that to get through my issues on my own because it isn't anyone else's business. If I knew then what I do now, perhaps life could have been different for me as well as so many people I've known throughout the years. There was such a stigma around mental health and I find there still is in this present day. Children and young teens need to know how important their feelings are as well as how important it is to address those feelings. As an adult I have learned that the sooner in life we can get these children and young adults to be open about how they feel, the sooner we can tackle those important issues.

Your perception of life is based on what you know growing up and what you see in the environment you are in. It sets the foundation at the early stages in life. Watching adults around you and how they handle their issues is what young children instill in themselves. It is hard to come out of the mentality that you can be different then what you know. Not many people realize that you can change and you can be better by taking care of yourself first. Many people I know thrive on taking care of others. But who takes care of them? I am not saying I'm against being there to support or help care for family members but what I am saying is that we all need help in one way or another. Sometimes taking on too much or even going through something takes a toll on our emotional wellbeing. What happens when music isn't enough? What do we do when writing in a journal is not helping? I urge anyone who is reading this book to find the courage and put yourself first. Your mental health is so important and it deserves to be taken care of. If you could take anything at all from reading this book, I hope it has encouraged you to take those important first steps in getting better mentally. If you do happen to need the help I once did, I hope I have encouraged you to be strong and put yourself first.

Updates!

My son Joseph Isaiah is now five years old and in kindergarten. I am doing great and still growing! I do still see a therapist every now and then to help me get through challenges I face along the way and I am very proud of myself for taking that first step and setting that appointment five years ago. I am now an advocate for mental health and motherhood. I am still married; we purchased our first home and added a puppy to the family. As I get older my passion for writing increases and it is to the point where I cannot neglect it any longer. I was able to take care of my mental health and now I am confident in taking care of my passions. My writing has not only always been a passion of mine but it is a calling. Currently I am working on a series of children's books to support the LGBT community because it is who I am and there is not enough support for families like mine. So why not use what I was blessed with to reach out to others all around the world. I am working hard to be the change I want to see in this world.

It took some time to write this book because it took me a little over two years to get back to my normal self. With taking my baby to get laser treatments and taking care of my mental health, it was a process. When I was pregnant, I began writing a journal. It was not a daily one but I tried to write in it as often as I can. The journal entries ceased after I gave birth. I have included the entries in this book because I promised I would be as open as I can with my readers. Plus I thought it would be fun to get an inside look at what I felt and thought throughout the pregnancy. I have always loved to write and have been doing it since as early on as I could remember. Lately I have wanted to reach out to mommies everywhere. I want mommies to know just how valuable they are and what we feel through our motherhood / parenting journey is natural and very important. We are not alone. You are not alone.

I thank you for being part of this journey with me. Stay tuned, as this is not the last you will hear from me.

Acknowledgements

I want to take this time to thank the people in my life who have encouraged me to do better for myself, hence this lovely read you have enjoyed.

I would like to express my deepest appreciation to my wife, Denise. We have been together in this journey we call life for over a decade and I thank you so much for pushing me to be at my best. There were times I did not understand your process or way of thinking but now that I can look at things in a different light, I want you to know that I appreciate you and the partnership you have offered throughout this time. For this, I will always love you.

To my beautiful and courageous mother, Virginia G., my life would not be what it is today if I did not have you. If I could ever take just one thing from every thing you have taught me it is to be strong. You have always said there is nothing stronger than a mother's love and now, I understand that.

Cesar – My confidant and my best friend in the world! Those late night talks did a number on my mental. You have helped me to see things in a totally different way. I have learned that spirituality is as important as breathing itself. So is being present in the moment and simply taking things for what they are. Thanks to you all I do is crave positive energy. I love you!

Peter – Words are not enough to say thank you for all you have done for me. Secretly you have become my mentor and someone that I look up to. You have kept me smiling in my darkest times and your love is something that doesn't come by often so I thank you and I cherish you forever and a day. You shed light on the importance of mental health but more importantly you lead by example. You my dearest friend are a force to be reckoned with!

I would also like to show appreciation to a few special people who have been there throughout the years even if just to offer advice, support or lend an ear to get me through my tough times as well as be present through the transitions and good times. Alyssa, Nicholas, Jessica, Cathy, Nayeli, Jeff, Doreen, Jem Jem and Chris.

Here is to my editor Talia Yarmush. I am grateful to have met you. I didn't know the first thing about making my dream a reality. It wasn't until I took your class on self-publishing that the pieces began to fit together. You believed in me before knowing me and pushed me to be a better writer. My gratitude towards you is immense.

Made in United States
North Haven, CT
18 October 2024

58624153R00085